THE POCKET
KEN WILBER

THE POCKET
KEN WILBER

Edited by

COLIN BIGELOW

SHAMBHALA
Boston & London
2008

Shambhala Publications, Inc.
Horticultural Hall
300 Massachusetts Avenue
Boston, Massachusetts 02115
www.shambhala.com

The Pocket Ken Wilber is an abridged and revised edition of
The Simple Feeling of Being: Embracing Your True Nature
(Shambhala, 2004).

See Sources, pages 169–177
for further copyright information.

9 8 7 6 5 4 3 2 1

First Edition

Printed in China

⊗ This edition is printed on acid-free paper that meets the
American National Standards Institute z39.48 Standard.

See page 181 for
Library of Congress Cataloging-in-Publication data.

To Mark Palmer, Sean Esbjörn-Hargens,
Vipassana Esbjörn-Hargens,
and Adam Leonard,
compilers and editors of Ken Wilber's
The Simple Feeling of Being,
of which this book is
a humble abridgement

CONTENTS

INTRODUCTION

WELCOME. It is my honor to introduce you to this compact tome of astonishing insight, compassion, and liberation. As Ken Wilber so eloquently summarized in the subtitle of one of his most recent books, *The Integral Vision*, his life work over more than three decades and two dozen books has explored and developed a "Revolutionary Integral Approach to Life, God, the Universe, and Everything." Speaking as his personal assistant, I think that is a very fine summary indeed. Speaking as his peer and colleague (ahem), I do believe he's forgotten a theme woven centrally into his entire philosophical canon: s-e-x. If I may say so (and I don't think I'm alone here), I personally believe sex is a deeply integral part of Life, God, the Universe, and Everything. It's rather hard to get a Kosmos going without it, yes? I mean, really, this all started with a *Big Bang*? Then a few billion years of subatomic particles enthusiastically colliding into each other, enacting a veritable orgy of substrate copulation, and POOF!, here we all are?

It appears that we humans are simply continuing this Kosmic tradition of colliding into one another, and quite often as creatively, eagerly, and frequently as possible. Well why not? After all, what is sex if not the active pursuit of uniting masculine and feminine energies (in whatever combination of bipeds we prefer) in a profound nondual integration, expressed—please god!—through a mind-blowing orgasm? I mean really, who *doesn't* see god at the point of full body/mind/soul climax? Who doesn't, in fact, feel that they might actually be *one* with spirit for those brief moments when the incessant stream of mental chatter is temporarily blown out of the water? *Who are you* when every ounce of your attention is racing towards, and finally achieves, an earth-shattering union with your lover in a timeless moment ripped open to infinity? That's right: you are the World—Life, God, the Universe, and Everything. Literally.

Through your recognition of the erotic in you, your desire to find unity in and through another being, you have found the doorway to the recognition of Eros in you. Eros is the universal force of the Kosmos incessantly driving towards, and *evolving* towards, greater wholeness, greater depth, greater union and integration. Your participation in the erotic is one way that Eros expresses itself in and through you. If you've read this far, you know—perhaps consciously admitting it to yourself for the first time—that as deeply as you may desire erotic union, you *powerfully* yearn for the

Ultimate union of self and Spirit that is your birthright. Not only is it your birthright, it is your true identity *right now*. This is the secret of the great mystical traditions: You have never been in exile, you have never left Home, you are literally One with the Real—right now. You are Spirit. You are God. You are Buddha Mind. You are Christ Consciousness. *You* are creating this entire universe moment-to-moment. (This is not narcissistic wish-fulfillment, whereby you, as a personal ego, finally get to have your dream career, a perfect relationship, and a fantastic body—that is a classic pre-conventional magical worldview, and clinging to this view is a guaranteed route to *not* realizing who you really are.) You are the Ultimate creative urge that brought forth—that literally birthed, through the passion of Spirit's infinite lust made manifest—all that is, all that was, and all there ever will be.

Hence, from the intensely Erotic impulse that animates and enlivens every cell in your body, and every atom in the universe . . . here we all are. Well done. Shall we explore in a little more detail all that You have created? Shall we learn a little more about the majesty springing forth from your own Self, mysteriously arising effortlessly, timelessly, in an ocean of infinite freedom?

What this unassuming little book contains is an introduction to the most complete map of the territory of you (and You) that the world has ever known. Needless to say, *the map is not the territory*, but that is not an excuse to have a crappy map. Looking at a map of Hawaii is not a substitute for actually being in Hawaii, but it will help you not get lost, and it will point out special items of interest—so the better the map, the more enjoyable your experience. Ken has literally spent his entire life trying to touch on all the bases of reality, and human life in particular, and then see how all those pieces fit together. Unfortunately, in today's cultural and academic atmosphere, the overwhelming emphasis is often on the *differences* in human cultures, subcultures, and historically marginalized groups of any kind. These differences are indeed real, and they must be respected, but when there is no attempt or even interest in finding *the patterns that connect*, the intrinsic basic features that humanity *shares*, then we are no longer a wildly diverse, radiant, holistic ornament of Spirit; we are shattered fragments of stained glass scattered across a gray and barren landscape, destined only to cut each other on the sharp edges of our stubborn demand to be the only special lens through which reality should shine, no matter how distorted or monochromatic that may be. This is what happens when pluralistic political correctness is taken to the extreme: everyone is equally special, and everyone is equally alienated, bleeding, and wondering why their special status leaves them feeling so miserable.

But it doesn't have to be that way. In fact, it isn't that way. The world just as it is, in all its fits and fury, *is* a perfect, whole, radiant ornament of Spirit. That is the Absolute nature of everything that is, even while manifesting as war, famine, genocide, poverty, despair, and all the slings and arrows of outrageous fortune. Our job, our purpose as conscious sentient beings, is to help this precious world of ours reflect ever more brightly the ultimate Radiance of the Real, and we do so by expressing the deepest level of wisdom and compassion we possibly can, to ease suffering and pain, to bring about joy and companionship, and to constantly seek to help people remember who they are, as the pure I AMness of Spirit, in this moment, and this, and this, endlessly and forever, in the eternal Eye of Spirit that we alone, in this precious human birth, can bring forth. It's up to us, together, and it shall always be so. What will you create in Spirit's own image, that is only and ever *you*?

Ken Wilber is a magnificent human being, it's true. By any meaningful definition, he is a genius of the first magnitude—hailed in exactly those words by literally dozens of his peers—whose canon of work not only continues to expand, but that has only continued to reinforce itself and hold together, from his very first book written when he was twenty-three (this, in the realm of philosophical discourse, is *extremely* rare). Many consider him a historic figure in his own time, and the work he is bringing forth will only continue to have more and more impact as the years and decades pass. It is not merely I that believes this: simply look at the Guest page on IntegralNaked.org, and the History page at

IntegralInstitute.org. But as someone who has known Ken intimately—in fact, daily—for more than five years, it is not him I want to celebrate. I want to celebrate YOU, and all that you can become. Because that is exactly what Ken's life's work is about, and will continue to be about. Ken is only ever pointing to *your own highest potentials*. So if you find any wisdom or insight in these pages, the greatest honor you could ever give to this loveable teddy-bear monument of a man is to claim that wisdom as your own, live by it, expand it, and share it with others.

Then, by whatever name, you will know what it means to be a Bodhisattva. You will know what it means to be a true disciple of Christ. You will know what it means to be an evolutionary instrument of Spirit.

Thus, I offer to you *The Pocket Ken Wilber*. May we meet one day, and recognize each other as the diamond sparkle of freshly fallen snow, the soft caress of a warm summer's breeze, the golden perfume of an autumn forest . . . and the quiet whisper of your breath as you read these words.

Even now, I am with you.

You see?

COLIN BIGELOW
Denver, Colorado, Winter 2008

THE POCKET
KEN WILBER

THE WITNESS

Within the deep silence of the great unborn, Spirit whispers a sublime secret, an otherwise hidden truth of one's very essence: You, in this and every moment, abide as Spirit itself, an immutable radiance beyond the mortal suffering of time and experience. Spirit itself is the very heart of one's own awareness, and it has always been so. Do you not remember this Self of yours, this great Witness? Is it not always your constant realization?

Notice first of all the broad, distinguishing marks of the transcendent self: it is a center and expanse of awareness which is creatively detached from one's personal mind, body, emotions, thoughts, and feelings. So if you would like to begin to work at intuiting this transcendent self within you that goes beyond you, the you that is not you, then proceed as follows:

Slowly begin to silently recite the following to yourself, trying to realize as vividly as possible the import of each statement:

I *have* a body, but I am *not* my body. I can see and feel my body, and what can be seen and felt is not the true Seer. My body may be tired or excited, sick or healthy, heavy or light, but that has nothing to do with my inward I. I *have* a body, but I am *not* my body.

I *have* desires, but I am *not* my desires. I can know my desires, and what can be known is not the true Knower. Desires come and go, floating through my awareness, but they do not affect my inward I. I *have* desires but I am *not* desires.

I *have* emotions, but I am *not* my emotions. I can feel and sense my emotions, and what can be felt and sensed is not the true

Feeler. Emotions pass through me, but they do not affect my inward I. I *have* emotions but I am *not* emotions.

I *have* thoughts, but I am *not* my thoughts. I can know and intuit my thoughts, and what can be known is not the true Knower. Thoughts come to me and thoughts leave me, but they do not affect my inward I. I *have* thoughts but I am *not* my thoughts.

This done—perhaps several times—one then affirms as concretely as possible: I am what remains, a pure center of awareness, an unmoved witness of all these thoughts, emotions, feelings, and desires.

If you persist at such an exercise, the understanding contained in it will quicken and you might begin to notice fundamental changes in your sense of "self." For example, you might begin intuiting a deep inward sense of freedom, lightness, release, stability. This source, this "center of the cyclone," will retain its lucid stillness even amid the raging winds of anxiety and suffering that might swirl around its center. The discovery of this witnessing center is very much like diving from the calamitous waves on the surface of a stormy ocean to the quiet and secure depths of the bottom. At first you might not get more than a few feet beneath the agitated waves of emotion, but with persistence you may gain the ability to dive fathoms into the quiet depths of your soul, and lying outstretched at the bottom, gaze up in alert but detached fashion at the turmoil that once held you transfixed.

Here we are talking of the transpersonal self or witness—we are not yet discussing pure unity consciousness. In unity consciousness, the transpersonal witness itself collapses into everything witnessed. Before that can occur, however, one must first discover that transpersonal witness, which then acts as an easier "jumping-off point" for unity consciousness. And we find this transpersonal witness by disidentifying with all particular objects, mental, emotional, or physical, thereby transcending them.

CW 1: *No Boundary*, 546–547

"WHO AM I?" The query has probably tormented humankind since the dawn of civilization, and remains today one of the most vexing of all human questions. Answers have been offered which range from the sacred to the profane, the complex to the simple, the scientific to the romantic, the political to the individual. But instead of examining the multitude of answers to this question, let's look instead at a very specific and basic process which occurs when a person asks, and then answers, the question "Who am I? What is my real self? What is my fundamental identity?"

When someone asks, "Who are you?"

and you proceed to give a reasonable, honest, and more or less detailed answer, what in fact, are you doing? What goes on in your head as you do this? In one sense you are describing your self as you have come to know it, including in your description most of the pertinent facts, both good and bad, worthy and worthless, scientific and poetic, philosophic and religious, that you understand as fundamental to your identity. You might, for example, think that "I am a unique person, a being endowed with certain potentials; I am kind but sometimes cruel, loving but sometimes hostile; I am a father and lawyer, I enjoy fishing and basketball. . . ." And so your list of feelings and thoughts might proceed.

Yet there is an even more basic process underlying the whole procedure of establishing an identity. Something very simple happens when you answer the question, "Who are you?" When you are describing or explaining or even just inwardly feeling your "self," what you are actually doing, whether you know it or not, is drawing a mental line or boundary across the whole field of your experience, and everything on the inside of that boundary you are feeling or calling your "self," while everything outside that boundary you feel to be "not-self." Your self-identity, in other words, depends entirely upon where you draw that boundary line.

You are a human and not a chair, and you know that because you consciously or unconsciously draw a boundary line between humans and chairs, and are able to recognize your identity with the former. You may be a very tall human instead of a short one; and so you draw a mental line between tallness and shortness, and thus identify yourself as "tall." You come to feel that "I am this and not that" by drawing a boundary line between "this" and "that" and then recognizing your identity with "this" and your nonidentity with "that."

So when you say "my self," you draw a boundary line between what is you and what is not you. When you answer the question, "Who are you?," you simply describe what's on the inside of that line. The so-called identity crisis occurs when you can't decide how or where to draw the line. In short, "Who are you?" means "Where do you draw the boundary?"

All answers to that question, "Who am I?," stem precisely from this basic procedure of drawing a boundary line between self and not-self. Once the general boundary lines have been drawn up, the answers to that question may become very complex—scientific, theological, economic— or they may remain most simple and unarticulated. But any possible answer depends on first drawing the boundary line.

The most interesting thing about this

boundary line is that it can and frequently does shift. It can be redrawn. In a sense the person can remap her soul and find in it territories she never thought possible, attainable, or even desirable. The most radical re-mapping or shifting of the boundary line occurs in experiences of the supreme identity, for here the person expands her self-identity boundary to include the entire universe. We might even say that she loses the boundary line altogether, for when she is identified with the "one harmonious whole" there is no longer any outside or inside, and so nowhere to draw the line.

CW 1: *No Boundary*, 435–437

THE WITNESS simply observes the stream of events both inside and outside the mind-body in a creatively detached fashion, since, in fact, the Witness is not exclusively identified with either. In other words, the individual realizes that his mind and his body can be perceived objectively, he spontaneously realizes that they cannot constitute a real subjective self.

CW 1: "Psychologia Perennis," 19

WHEN, AS a specific type of meditation, you pursue the observing Self, the Witness, to its very *source* in pure Emptiness, then no objects arise in consciousness at all. This is a discrete, identifiable state of awareness—namely, *unmanifest absorption* or *cessation*, variously known as nirvikalpa samadhi, jnana samadhi, ayin, vergezzen, nirodh, classical nirvana, the cloud of unknowing.

This is the causal state, a discrete state, which is often likened to the state of deep dreamless sleep, except that this state is not a mere blank but rather an utter fullness, and it is experienced as such—as infinitely drenched in the fullness of Being, so full that no manifestation can even begin to contain it. Because it can never be seen as an object, this pure Self is pure Emptiness.

CW 7: *A Brief History of Everything*, 251

THE CONTEMPLATIVE traditions are based on a series of experiments in awareness: what if you pursue this Witness to its source? What if you inquire within, pushing deeper and deeper into the source of awareness itself? What if you push beyond or behind the mind, into a depth of consciousness that is not confined to the ego or the individual self? What do you find? As a repeatable, reproducible experiment in awareness, what do you find?

"There is a subtle essence that pervades all reality," begins one of the most famous answers to that question. "It is the reality of all that is, and the foundation of all that is.

That essence is all. That essence is the real. And thou, thou art that."

In other words, this observing Self eventually discloses its own source, which is Spirit itself, Emptiness itself. And that is why the mystics maintain that this observing Self is a ray of the Sun that is the radiant Abyss and ultimate Ground upon which the entire manifest Kosmos depends. Your very Self intersects the Self of the Kosmos at large—a supreme identity that outshines the entire manifest world, a supreme identity that undoes the knot of the separate self and buries it in splendor.

So from matter to body to mind to Spirit. In each case consciousness or the observing Self sheds an exclusive identity with a lesser and shallower dimension, and opens up to deeper and higher and wider occasions, until it opens up to its own ultimate ground in Spirit itself.

And the stages of transpersonal growth

and development are basically the stages of following this observing Self to its ultimate abode, which is pure Spirit or pure Emptiness, the ground, path, and fruition of the entire display.

CW 7: *A Brief History of Everything*,
232–233

RAMANA [MAHARSHI], echoing Shankara, used to say:

The world is illusory;
Brahman alone is real;
Brahman is the world.

The world is illusory, which means you are not any object at all—nothing that can be seen is ultimately real. You are *neti, neti*, not this, not that. And under no circumstances should you base your salvation on that which is finite, temporal, passing, illusory, suffering-enhancing and agony-inducing.

Brahman alone is real, the Self (unqualifiable Brahman-Atman) alone is real—the pure Witness, the timeless Unborn, the formless Seer, the radical I-I, radiant Emptiness—is what is real and all that is real. It is your condition, your nature, your essence, your present and your future, your desire and your destiny, and yet it is always ever-present as pure Presence, the alone that is Alone.

Brahman is the world, Emptiness and Form are not-two. *After* you realize that the manifest world is illusory, and *after* you realize that Brahman alone is real, *then* you can see that the absolute and the relative are not-two or nondual, then you can see that nirvana and samsara are not-two, then you can realize that the Seer and everything seen are not-two, Brahman and the world are not-two—all of which really means, the sound of those birds singing! The entire world of Form exists no-where but in your own present Formless Awareness: you can drink the Pacific in a single gulp, because the entire world literally exists in your pure Self, the ever-present great I-I.

Finally, and most important, Ramana would remind us that the pure Self—and therefore the great Liberation—*cannot be attained*, any more than you can attain your feet or acquire your lungs. You are *already* aware of the sky, you *already* hear the sounds around you, you *already* witness this world. One hundred percent of the enlightened mind or pure Self is present right now—not ninety-nine percent, but one hundred percent. As Ramana constantly pointed out, if the Self (or knowledge of the Self) is something that comes into existence—if your realization has a beginning in time—then that is merely another object, another passing, finite, temporal state. There is no reaching the Self—the Self is reading this page. There is no looking for the Self—it is looking out of your eyes right now. There is no attaining the Self—it is reading these words. You simply, absolutely, cannot attain that which you have never lost. And if you do attain something, Ramana would say, that's very nice, but that's not the Self.

So, if I may suggest, as you read the following words from the world's greatest sage: if you think you don't understand Self or Spirit, then rest in that which doesn't understand, and just that is Spirit. If you think you don't quite "get" the Self or Spirit, then rest in that which doesn't quite get it, and just that is Spirit.

Thus, if you think you understand Spirit, that is Spirit. If you think you don't, that is Spirit. And so we can leave with Ramana's greatest and most secret message: the enlightened mind is not hard to attain but impossible to avoid. In the dear Master's words:

There is neither creation nor destruction,
Neither destiny nor free-will;
Neither path nor achievement;
This is the final truth.

CW 8: *One Taste,* 465–468

TRULY, ADOPTING a new holistic philosophy, believing in Gaia, or even thinking in integral terms—however important those might be, they are the least important when it comes to spiritual transformation. Finding out who believes in all those things: There is the doorway to God.

A Theory of Everything, 137

THE SOUL, as I am using the term, is a sort of halfway house, halfway between the personal ego-mind and the impersonal or transpersonal Spirit. The soul is the Witness as it shines forth in you and nobody else.

The soul is the home of the Witness in that sense. Once you are established on the soul level, then you are established as the Witness, as the real Self. Once you push through the soul level, then the Witness itself collapses into everything witnessed, or you become one .with everything you are aware of. You don't witness the clouds, you are the clouds. That's Spirit. . . .

In a sense the soul or the Witness in you is the highest pointer toward Spirit and the last barrier to Spirit. It's only from the position of the Witness that you can jump into Spirit, so to speak. But the Witness itself eventually has to dissolve or die. Even your own soul has to be sacrificed and released and let go of, or died to, in order for your ultimate identity with Spirit to radiate forth. Because ultimately the soul is just the final contraction in awareness, the subtlest knot restricting universal Spirit, the last and subtlest form of the separate-self sense, and that final knot has to be undone. That's the last death, as it were. First we die to the material self—that is, disidentify with it— then we die to an exclusive identity with the bodily self, then to the mental self, and then finally to the soul. The last one is what Zen calls the Great Death.

CW 5: *Grace and Grit*, 120–121

[SRI RAMANA] Maharshi's unique contribution to the ways of liberation is his insistence that the "I-thought" is the source of all other thoughts. That is, every time you think of your "self," that is the I-thought, and Ramana declares it to lie behind every other thought:

> The first and foremost of all the thoughts that arise in the mind is the primal "I"-thought. It is only after the rise or origin of the "I"-thought that innumerable other thoughts arise.

Thus the suspension of the I-thought marks the suspension of all other thoughts and mental objects. Now Sri Ramana Maharshi realizes that the I-thought cannot be suppressed—for who would suppress "I" except another "I"? Spiritual altruism is spiritual hypocrisy. The I-thought, like any other thought, is to be suspended, not suppressed, and for this suspension, Ramana recommends what he calls "Self-Inquiry (*nan yar*)," which is the intensively active inquiry "Who am I?" . . .

How does this self-inquiry work? Let us suppose, for example, that I ask you, "Who are you?" and you reply, "Well, I am so-and-so, I work at this particular job, I'm married, and I am of such-and-such religion. Is that what you mean?" "No," I would answer, "those are all objects of perception, they are mere ideas. Who are you that sees these objects, these ideas?" "Well, I am a human being, an individual organism endowed with certain biological faculties. Is that closer?" "Not really," I would have to counter, "for those are still ideas and thoughts. Now deeply, *who are you?*" As your mind keeps turning back in on itself in search of the answer, it gets quieter and quieter. If I kept asking "Who are you? Who are you?" you would quickly enter a mental silence, and that mental silence would be identical to the one produced by Benoit's question, "How do you feel from all possible views at once?" That *object-less silence* produced by active attention, by vigilant watchfulness, by intense inquiry, is a Bodhimandala, for right at the point where no mental answer, image, or object is forthcoming, you are open to seeing the Real in a flash.

CW 1: *The Spectrum of Consciousness*, 351–353

PEOPLE TYPICALLY feel trapped by life, trapped by the universe, because they imagine that they are actually *in* the universe, and therefore the universe can squish them like a bug. This is not true. You are not in the universe; the universe is in you.

The typical orientation is this: my consciousness is in my body (mostly in my head); my body is in this room; this room is in the surrounding space, the universe itself. That is true from the viewpoint of the ego, but utterly false from the viewpoint of the Self.

If I rest as the Witness, the formless I-I, it becomes obvious that, right now, I am not in my body, my body is IN my awareness. I am aware of my body, therefore I am not my body. I am the pure Witness in which my body is now arising. I am not in my body, my body is in my consciousness. Therefore, *be* consciousness.

If I rest as the Witness, the formless I-I, it becomes obvious that, right now, I am not in this house, this house is IN my awareness. I am the pure Witness in which this house is now arising. I am not in this house, this house is in my consciousness. Therefore, *be* consciousness.

If I look outside this house, to the surrounding area—perhaps a large stretch of earth, a big patch of sky, other houses, roads and cars—if I look, in short, at the universe in front of me—and if I rest as the Witness, the formless I-I, it becomes obvious that, right now, I am not in the universe, the universe is IN my awareness. I am the pure Witness in which this universe is now arising. I am not in the universe, the universe is in my consciousness. Therefore, *be* consciousness.

It is true that the physical matter of your body is inside the matter of the house, and the matter of the house is inside the matter of the universe. But you are not merely matter or physicality. You are also Consciousness as Such, of which matter is merely the outer skin. The ego adopts the viewpoint of matter, and therefore is constantly trapped by matter—trapped and tortured by the physics of pain. But pain, too, arises in your consciousness, and you can either be in pain, or find pain in you, so that you surround pain, are bigger than pain, transcend pain, as you rest in the vast expanse of pure Emptiness that you deeply and truly are.

So what do I see? If I contract as ego, it appears that I am confined in the body, which is confined in the house, which is confined in the large universe around it. But if I rest as the Witness—the vast, open, empty consciousness—it becomes obvious that I am not in the body, the body is in me; I am not in this house, the house is in me; I am not in the universe, the universe is in me. All of them are arising in the vast, open, empty, pure, luminous Space of primordial Consciousness, right now and right now and forever right now.

Therefore, *be* Consciousness.

CW 8: *One Taste*, 448–449

2

SPIRIT-IN-ACTION

One thing that characterizes Ken Wilber's integral vision is his skill in articulating the evolutionary dynamics of Spirit's unfolding in time and through space. In the following selections, Wilber traces the choreography of the dance in which Heaven and Earth are engaged: how Heaven throws itself out of the Abyss creating Earth, and how Earth reaches ever upward toward Heaven. These selections reveal a dedicated exploration and straightforward explanation of this ebb and flow of the Divine cascading into and out of form. Whether discussing Ascent into the sky and Descent toward soil or Eros's drive toward wholeness and Agape's embrace of the many, Wilber always poetically describes the relationship between development and stillness: Spirit's Longing to incarnate and Matter's desire to be God.

EVOLUTION IS best thought of as *Spirit-in-action*, God-in-the-making, where Spirit unfolds itself at every stage of development, thus manifesting more of itself, and realizing more of itself, at every unfolding. Spirit is not some particular stage, or some favorite ideology, or some specific god or goddess, but rather the entire process of unfolding itself, an infinite process that is completely present at every finite stage, but becomes more available to itself with every evolutionary opening.

CW 7: *A Brief History of Everything*, 61

EMPTINESS ALONE, only and all, with an edge of extremely faint yet luminous bliss. That is how the subtle feels when it emerges from the causal. So it was early this morning. As the gross body then emerges from this subtle luminous bliss it's hard to tell, at first, exactly where its boundaries are. You have a body, you know that, but the body seems like the entire material universe. Then the bedroom solidifies, and slowly, very slowly, your awareness accepts the conventions of the gross realm, which dictate that *this* body is inside *this* room. And so it is. And so you get up. And so goes involution, yet again.

But the Emptiness remains, always.

CW 8: *One Taste*, 410

BEING AND CONSCIOUSNESS exist as a spectrum, reaching from matter to body to mind to soul to Spirit. And although Spirit is, in a certain sense, the highest dimension or level of the spectrum of existence, it is also the ground or condition of the entire spectrum. It is as if Spirit were both the highest rung on the ladder of existence *and* the wood out of which the entire ladder is made—Spirit is both totally and com-

pletely immanent (as the wood) and totally
and completely transcendent (as the highest rung). Spirit is both Ground and Goal.

In its immanent aspect, Spirit is the Condition of all conditions, the Being of all beings, the Nature of all natures. As such, it
neither evolves nor involves, grows or develops, ascends or descends. It is the simple
suchness or isness—the perfect isness—of
all that is, of each and every thing in manifestation. There is no contacting immanent
Spirit, no way to reach It, no way to com-
mune with It, for there is nothing It is not.
Being completely and totally present at
every single point of space and time, It is
fully and completely present here and now,
and thus we can no more attain immanent
Spirit than we could, say, attain our feet.

In its transcendental aspect, however,
Spirit is the highest rung on our own ladder
of growth and evolution. It is something we
must work to comprehend, to understand,

to attain union with, to identify with. The realization of our Supreme Identity with Spirit dawns only after much growth, much development, much evolution, and much inner work—only then do we understand that the Supreme Identity was there, from the beginning, perfectly given in its fullness. In other words, it is only from the highest rung on the ladder that we can realize the wood out of which the entire ladder is made.

It is this paradox of Spirit—both fully present (as the Ground of Being) and yet to be realized (as our highest Goal)—that lies behind such paradoxical Zen sayings as:

If there is any discipline toward reaching Spirit, then the completion of that discipline means the destruction of Spirit. But if there is no discipline toward Spirit, one remains an ignoramus.

In other words, while in its immanent aspects Spirit simply *is*, in its transcendental aspects Spirit evolves or develops. The entire manifest world, while remaining fully and completely grounded in Spirit, is also struggling to awaken Spirit in itself, struggling to realize Spirit *as* Spirit, struggling to arouse from the nightmare of time and stand strong in eternity. This struggle of growth and development appears in the world at large as evolution, and in individual men and women as the growth and development of their own consciousness (which is simply the arena of cosmic evolution in human beings). Evolution is the movement of Spirit, toward Spirit, as Spirit, the conscious resurrection, in all men and women, of the Supreme Identity, an Identity present all along, but an Identity seemingly obscured by manifestation, seemingly obscured by the limited view from a lower rung on the ladder. As one intuits the higher and highest rungs of the ladder of existence, Spirit sees Itself as Spirit, sees Itself everywhere, sees there was never a time that It wasn't—and then, but only then, is the entire ladder thrown away, now having served its manifest purpose. And one understands, in the entire process, that not a single thing has been attained.

CW 1: *The Spectrum of Consciousness*, 43–44

ACCORDING TO the perennial philosophy—or the common core of the world's great wisdom traditions—Spirit manifests a universe by "throwing itself out" or "emptying itself" to create soul, which condenses into mind, which condenses into body, which condenses into matter, the densest form of all. Each of those levels is still a level of Spirit, but each is a reduced or "stepped-down" version of Spirit. At the end of that process of *involution*, all of the higher dimensions are enfolded, as potential, in the lowest material realm. And once the material world blows into existence (with, say, the Big Bang), then the reverse process—or evolution—can occur, moving from matter to living bodies to symbolic minds to luminous souls to pure Spirit itself. In this developmental or evolutionary unfolding, each successive level does not jettison or deny the previous level, but rather includes and embraces it, just as atoms are included in molecules, which are included in cells, which are included in organisms. Each level is a whole that is also part of a larger whole (each level or structure is a whole/part or holon). In other words, each evolutionary unfolding transcends but includes its predecessor(s), with Spirit transcending and including absolutely everything.

This arrangement—Spirit transcends

but includes soul, which transcends but includes mind, which transcends but includes body, which transcends but includes matter—is often referred to as the Great Chain of Being, but that is clearly a very unfortunate misnomer. Each successive level is not a link but a nest, which includes, embraces, and envelops its predecessor(s). The Great Chain of Being is really the Great Nest of Being—not a ladder, chain, or one-way hierarchy, but a series of concentric spheres of increasing holistic embrace.

CW 2: *Introduction*, 10

REALITY IS not composed of things or processes; it is not composed of atoms or quarks; it is not composed of wholes nor does it have any parts. Rather, it is composed of whole/parts, or holons.

This is true of atoms, cells, symbols, ideas. They can be understood neither as things nor processes, neither as wholes nor parts, but only as simultaneous whole/parts, so that standard "atomistic" and "wholistic" attempts are both off the mark. There is nothing that isn't a holon (upwardly and downwardly forever).

Before an atom is an atom, it is a holon. Before a cell is a cell, it is a holon. Before an idea is an idea, it is a holon. All of them are wholes that exist in other wholes, and thus they are all whole/parts, or holons, first and foremost (long before any "particular characteristics" are singled out by us).

Likewise, reality might indeed be composed of processes and not things, but all processes are only processes within other processes—that is, they are first and foremost holons. Trying to decide whether the fundamental units of reality are things or processes is utterly beside the point, because either way, they are all holons, and centering on one or the other misses the central issue. Clearly some things exist, and some processes exist, but they are each and all holons.

Therefore we can examine what *holons* have in common, and this releases us from the utterly futile attempt to find common processes or common entities on all levels and domains of existence, because that will never work; it leads always to reductionism, not true synthesis.

For example, to say that the universe is composed primarily of quarks is already to privilege a particular domain. Likewise, at the other end of the spectrum, to say that the universe is really composed primarily of our symbols, since these are all we really know—that, too, is to privilege a particular domain. But to say that the universe is composed of holons neither privileges a domain nor implies special fundamentalness for any level. Literature, for example, is *not* composed of subatomic particles; but both literature and subatomic particles are composed of holons.

CW 6: *Sex, Ecology, Spirituality*, 41–42

THE DIFFERENT levels of the spectrum are something like the various waves of the ocean—each wave is certainly different from all others. Some waves, near the shore, are strong and powerful; while others, farther out, are weaker and less powerful. But each wave is still different from all the others, and if you were surfing you could select a particular wave, catch it, ride it, and work it according to your ability. You couldn't do any of this if the waves weren't different. Each level of the spectrum is like a particular wave, and thus we can "catch" any of them with the right technique and enough practice.

Unity consciousness, however, is not so much a particular wave as it is the *water* itself. And there is no boundary, no difference, no separation between water and any of the waves. That is, the water is equally present in *all* waves, in the sense that no wave is wetter than another.

So if you are looking for "wetness" itself—the *condition* of all waves—nothing whatsoever will be gained by jumping from one wave to another. In fact, there is much to lose, for as long as you are wave-jumping in search of wetness, you obviously will never discover that wetness exists in its purity on whatever wave you're riding now. Seeking unity consciousness is like jumping from one wave of experience to another in search of water. And that is why "there is neither path nor achievement."

CW 1: *No Boundary*, 559

EVOLUTION—wherever it appears—manifests itself as a series of transcendences, of ascents, of emergences—and emergences of higher-order *wholes*. For to remember is really to re-member, or join again in unity, and that is just why evolution consists of a series of ever-higher wholes until there is only Wholeness. Evolution is holistic because it is nature's remembrance of God.

CW 2: *The Atman Project*, 267

THE NOTION of evolution as Eros, or Spirit-in-action, performing, as Whitehead put it, throughout the world by gentle persuasion toward love, goes a long way to explaining the inexorable unfolding from matter to bodies to minds to souls to Spirit's own Self-recognition. Eros, or Spirit-in-action, is a rubber band around your neck and mine, pulling us all back home.

CW 2: *Introduction*, 12

LOOK AT the course of evolution to date: from amoebas to humans! Now, what if that ratio, amoebas to humans, were applied to future evolution? That is, amoebas are to humans as humans are to—what? Is it ridiculous to suggest that the "what" might indeed be omega, *geist*, supermind, spirit? That Brahman is not only the *ground* of evolution but the *goal* as well?

CW 3: *A Sociable God*, 446

AND SO proceeds meditation, which is simply higher development, which is simply higher evolution—a transformation from unity to unity until there is simple Unity, whereupon Brahman, in an unnoticed shock of recognition and final remembrance, grins silently to itself, closes its eyes, breathes deeply, and throws itself outward for the millionth time, losing itself in its manifestations for the sport and play of all. Evolution then proceeds again, transformation by transformation, remembering more and more, unifying more and more, until every soul remembers Buddha, as Buddha, in Buddha—whereupon there is then no Buddha and no soul. And that is the final transformation. When Zen master Fa-ch'ang was dying, a squirrel screeched on the roof. "It's just this," he said, "and nothing more."

CW 3: *Eye to Eye*, 263

MYSTICISM IS transrational and thus lies in our collective future, not our collective past. Mysticism is evolutionary and progressive, not devolutionary and regressive, as Aurobindo and Teilhard de Chardin realized. And science, in my opinion, is stripping us of our infantile and adolescent views of spirit, is stripping us of our prerational views, in order to make room for the genuinely transrational insights of the higher stages of development, the transpersonal stages of genuine mystical or contemplative development. It is stripping magic and mythic in order to make room for psychic and subtle. In that sense science (and rationality) is a very healthy, very evolutionary, very necessary step toward real spiritual maturity. Rationality is a movement *of* spirit *toward* spirit.

CW 5: *Grace and Grit*, 234

EVERY STAGE of development liberates the Witness from a previous identification: symbols witness images, concepts witness symbols, rules witness concepts, and so forth.

CW 6: *Sex, Ecology, Spirituality*, 637

THE GREAT GODDESS is best conceived, not as any particular structure or epoch or nature, horticultural or otherwise, but as the overall movement of Efflux, of Creative Descent and Superabundance, of Agape and Goodness and Compassion. She is not Gaia, not nature, not planting mythology (although She embraces all of those in Her divinely Creative Matrix). She even embraces the patriarchy and was every bit as much behind that structure as any other. (Likewise, true God is not the Great Father figure, but the overall movement of Reflux and Ascent and Eros . . .)

By confusing the Great Goddess with the horticultural Great Mother mythic corpus—which was indeed *superseded* with the coming of the patriarchy—it appears that male culture destroyed the Goddess (a handful of males on a small planet destroyed the Creative Efflux of the entire Kosmos?), and that what is required is a recovery and resurrection of the Great Mother mythos.

The same Zoroastrian dualism, the same assumption that the Goddess *could* be banished, when all that was banished was a poorly differentiated mythos that many ecofeminists have reinterpreted to fit their ideology. When the Great Goddess is instead seen to be the entire movement of Creative Descent and Efflux (at each and every epoch), then the cure is no longer regression to horticultural mythology, but progression to Goddess embodiment in the forms of today's integrations (Agape).

The Great Goddess is not a victim, nor could She be banished without destroying the entire manifest universe. But by claiming that She was banished, and by purporting to know how and why it happened, these ecofeminists are then in possession of a certain type of power, the power to tell the world what it must do in order to recapture an ethos of which these theorists are now the primary possessors. The Goddess is shackled to a horticultural planting mythology that ensures that She could never be integrated with modernity, and sees Her only as our Lady of the Eternal Victim. The very framing of the Goddess in those terms denies Her ever-present creative attributes and buries them in rhetoric.

That which one can deviate from is not the true Tao. Not only is modernity not devoid of the Goddess, her Goodness and Agape and Compassion are written all over it, with its radically new and emergent stance of worldcentric pluralism, universal benevolence, and multicultural tolerance, something that no horticultural society could even conceive, let alone implement. Her Grace grows stronger and more obvious with every gain in the liberation movements, and that we ourselves have not always lived up to her new Grace that was modernity's Enlightenment, shows only that we are still surly children not on speaking terms with our own divine parents.

CW 6: *Sex, Ecology, Spirituality*, 692–693

HUMAN BEINGS are born and begin their evolution through the great spiral of consciousness, moving from archaic to magic to mythic to rational to . . . perhaps integral, and perhaps from there into genuinely transpersonal domains. But for every person that moves into integral or higher, dozens are born into the archaic. The spiral of existence is a great unending flow, stretching from body to mind to soul to spirit, with millions upon millions constantly flowing through that great river from source to ocean.

CW 7: *A Brief History of Everything*, 35

The Masculine Face of Spirit—or God—is preeminently Eros, the Ascending and *transcendental* current of the Kosmos, ever-striving to find greater wholeness and wider unions, to break the limits and reach for the sky, to rise to unending revelations of a greater Good and Glory, always rejecting the shallower in search of the deeper, rejecting the lower in search of the higher.

And the Feminine Face of Spirit—the Goddess—is preeminently Agape, or Compassion, the Descending and *immanent* and manifesting current of the Kosmos, the principle of embodiment, and bodily incarnation, and relationship, and relational and manifest embrace, touching each and every being with perfect and equal grace, rejecting nothing, embracing all. Where Eros strives for the Good of the One in transcendental wisdom, Agape embraces the Many with Goodness and immanent care.

CW 7: *A Brief History of Everything*, 284

BECAUSE SPIRIT manifests equally in all four quadrants, or equally in the Big Three, then we can describe Spirit *subjectively* as one's own Buddha-mind—the "I" of Spirit, the Beauty. And we can describe Spirit *objectively* as Dharma—the "It" of Spirit, the ultimate Truth. And we can describe Spirit *culturally* as Sangha—the "We" of Spirit, the ultimate Good.

These four quadrants, or the Big Three, are all facets of Spirit, facets of Emptiness. When Emptiness manifests, it does so as subject and object, each of which can be singular or plural. And that gives us the four quadrants, or simply the Big Three. So Spirit can be described—and must be described—with all three languages, I and we and it.

Each of those domains evolves. Which means, each unfolds its spiritual nature more and more, and thus realizes its spiritual nature more and more. And in the uppermost reaches of that evolution, the I and the We and the It increasingly become transparent to their own true nature. They each radiate the glory of the Ground that they are.

And in that radiant awareness, every I becomes a God, and every We becomes God's sincerest worship, and every It becomes God's most gracious temple.

CW 7: *A Brief History of Everything*, 174

FOR AQAL, the quadrants, or simply the Big 3 (I, You/We, It), go all the way down and all the way up. As soon as there is any sort of manifestation, even causal, or as soon as Spirit itself first manifests in existence, there is Spirit in 1st-person, Spirit in 2nd-person, and Spirit in 3rd-person.

Spirit in 1st-person is the great I, the I-I, the Maha-Atman, the Overmind—Spirit as that great Witness in you, the I-I of this and every moment. The very Witness *in which* this page is arising, and this room, and this universe, this Witness or I-I in you is Spirit in its 1st-person mode.

Spirit in 2nd-person is the great You, the great Thou, the radiant, living, all-giving God before whom I must surrender in love and devotion and sacrifice and release. In the face of Spirit in 2nd-person, in the face of the God who is All Love, I can have only one response: to find God in this moment, I must love until it hurts, love to infinity, love until there is no me left anywhere, only this radiant living Thou who bestows all glory, all goods, all knowledge, all grace, and forgives me deeply for my own manifestation, which inherently brings suffering to others, but which the loving God of the Thou-ness of this moment can and does release, forgive, heal, and make whole, but only if I can surrender in the core of my being, surrender the self-contraction through love and devotion and care and conscious-ness, surrender to the great Thou, as God or Goddess, but here and now, radiant and always, this something-that-is-always-greater-than-me, and which discloses the depths of this moment that are beyond the I and me and mine, beyond the self alto-gether, and given to me by the Thou-ness of this moment, but only if I can deeply and radically surrender in love and devotion to the Great-Thou dimension of this now. This Great God/dess that *faces me* right now, that is *talking to me* right now, that is *revealing* Him/Herself to me as a communion with Thou in a sacred we, is Spirit in its 2nd-per-son mode.

Spirit in 3rd-person is the Great It, or Great System, or Great Web of Life, the Great Perfection of existence itself, the Is-ness, the Thus-ness, the very Such-ness of this and every moment. Spirit arises in its 3rd-person mode as this vast impersonal evolutionary System, the great Interlocking Order, the Great Holarchy of Being, of interconnected planes and levels and spheres and orders, stretching from dust to Deity, from dirt to Divinity, but all nonetheless in the Great Perfection of the unfolding suchness of this moment, and this moment, and this. All of those conceptions are 3rd-person conceptions, or Spirit in its 3rd-person mode.

Integral Spirituality, 158–159

ALL SUCH attempts [at formulating a theory of everything], of course, are marked by the many ways in which they fail. The many ways in which they fall short, make unwarranted generalizations, drive specialists insane, and generally fail to achieve their stated aim of holistic embrace. It's not just that the task is beyond any one human mind; it's that the task itself is inherently undoable: knowledge expands faster than ways to categorize it. The holistic quest is an ever-receding dream, a horizon that constantly retreats as we approach it, a pot of gold at the end of a rainbow that we will never reach.

So why even attempt the impossible? Because, I believe, a little hit of wholeness is better than none at all, and an integral vision offers considerably more wholeness than the slice-and-dice alternatives. We can be more whole, or less whole; more fragmented, or less fragmented; more alienated, or less alienated—and an integral vision invites us to be a little more whole, a little less fragmented, in our work, our lives, our destiny.

A Theory of Everything: XII

WE CAN therefore summarize Plato's overall position in words that would apply to any Nondual stance wherever it appears: flee the Many, find the One; having found the One, embrace the Many *as* the One.

Or, in short: Return to One, embrace Many.

CW 6: *Sex, Ecology, Spirituality*, 336

PHYSICS, in short, deals with—and can only deal with—the world of shadow-symbols, not the light of reality beyond the shadowy cave . . .

Both the old and the new physics were dealing with shadow-symbols, *but the new physics was forced to be aware of that fact*—forced to be aware that it was dealing with shadows and illusions, not reality. . . .

There is the great difference between the old and new physics—both are dealing with shadows, but the old physics didn't recognize that fact. If you are *in* the cave of shadows and don't even know it, then of course you have no reason or desire to try to escape to the light beyond. The shadows appear to be the whole world, and no other reality is acknowledged or even suspected—this tended to be the philosophic effect of the old physics. But with the new physics, the shadowy character of the whole enterprise became much more obvious, and sensitive physicists by the droves began to look beyond the cave (and beyond physics) altogether . . .

To put it in a nutshell: according to this view, physics deals with shadows; to go beyond shadows is to go beyond physics; to go beyond physics is to head toward the metaphysical or mystical—and *that* is why so many of our pioneering physicists were mystics. The new physics contributed nothing positive to this mystical venture, except a spectacular failure, from whose smoking ruins the spirit of mysticism gently arose.

CW 4: *Quantum Questions*, 252—255

SPIRIT OR Godhead, when apprehended by the mind, is a paradox: both Goal and Ground, Source and Summit, Alpha and Omega. *From the view of Ground*, history *is* pure illusion. Since God is equally and wholly present at every point of time, then history can neither add to nor subtract from God's omnipresence. *From the view of Summit or Goal*, however, history *is* the unfolding of God to Itself, or the movement from subconscious to selfconscious to superconscious modes; only the latter or superconscient mode can *directly realize* an everpresent unity with God-as-Ground, and thus the latter *alone*, of all the modes, is the direct realization *of* God *by* God. From that point of view, history is the unfolding of God to Itself, an unfolding that appears to us, through a glass darkly, as evolution. From this side of the paradox, history is no mere illusion, *it is the very sub-*

stance of this drama and the very means of its enactment.

CW 4: "Sociocultural Evolution," 337

WE DIG within in order to go beyond, not back.

CW 4: *Integral Psychology*, 534

WITH SPIRIT'S shocking Self-recognition, Forms continue to arise and evolve, but the secret is out: they are all Forms of Emptiness in the universe of One Taste, endlessly transparent and utterly Divine. There is no end limit, no foundation, no final resting place, only Emptiness and endless Grace. So the luminous Play carries on with insanely joyous regard, timeless gesture to timeless gesture, radiant in its wild release, ecstatic in its perfect abandon, endless fullness beyond endless fullness, this miraculously self-liberating Dance, and there is no one anywhere to watch it, or even sing its praises.

CW 7: *A Brief History of Everything*, 276

GOD DOES not lie in our collective past, God lies in our collective future; the Garden of Eden is tomorrow, not yesterday; the Golden Age lies down the road, not up it.

CW 7: *The Eye of Spirit*, 475

THERE IS a new koan for our age, and only the neoperennial philosophy can answer it: Does a computer have Buddha-nature?

CW 7: *The Eye of Spirit*, 475

THE PAST has the Great Religions. The future will have the Greater Religions.

CW 7: *The Eye of Spirit*, 477

SPIRIT KNOWS itself objectively as Nature; knows itself subjectively as Mind; and knows itself absolutely as Spirit—the Source, the Summit, the Ground, and the Process of the entire ordeal.

CW 8: *The Marriage of Sense and Soul*, 175

SPIRIT IS *unfolding* itself in each new transcendence, which it also *enfolds* into its own being at the new stage. Transcends and includes, brings forth and embraces, creates and loves, Eros and Agape, unfolds and enfolds—different ways of saying the same thing.

So we can summarize all this very simply: because evolution *goes beyond* what went before, but because it must *embrace* what went before, then its very nature is to transcend and include, and thus it has an inherent directionality, a secret impulse, toward increasing depth, increasing intrinsic value, increasing consciousness. In order for evolution to move at all, it must move in those directions—there's no place else for it to go!

CW 7: *A Brief History of Everything*, 89–90

BECAUSE [THE] Nondual condition is the nature or suchness of any and all states— because this Emptiness is one with whatever Forms arise—then the world of Form will continue to arise, and you will continue to relate to Form. You will not try to get out of it, or away from it, or suspend it. You will enter it fully.

And since Forms continue to arise, then you are *never* at an *end point* where you can say, "Here, I am fully Enlightened." In these traditions, Enlightenment is an ongoing process of new Forms arising, and you relate to them as Forms of Emptiness. You are one with all these Forms as they arise. And in that sense, you are "enlightened," but in another sense, this enlightenment is *ongoing*, because new Forms are arising all the time. You are never in a *discrete* state that has no further development. You are always learning new things about the world of Form, and therefore your overall state is always evolving itself.

So you can have certain breakthrough Enlightenment experiences—satori, for example—but these are just the *beginning* of an *endless* process of riding the new waves of Form as they ceaselessly arise. So in this sense, in the Nondual sense, you are never "fully" Enlightened, any more than you could say that you are "fully educated." It has no meaning.

CW 7: *A Brief History of Everything*, 267–268

IN A SENSE, the nondual realization for a fair number of people right around the turn of the century, including Sri Aurobindo, is still unfolding. I mean, the world of form keeps unfolding, keeps evolving—spirit's own self-expression keeps unfolding—and it happens, as far as we can tell, to build on what it did yesterday, which is why evolution is indeed an unfolding event in the world of form. So as this incarnational non-duality, this ultimately ecstatic tantric non-duality itself, began to unfold, and its forms of manifestation began to unfold, you find that by the time you get to people like Sri Aurobindo, there's such a full-bodied understanding of this process. Even though some of the earlier sages were ultimately enlightened for their time, there's a richness, an unfolding, a resonance of spirit's own incarnational understanding in some of these recent sages that just gives you goosebumps.

If we talk about enlightenment as the union of emptiness and form, the pure emptiness doesn't change because it doesn't enter the stream of time, but the form does change, and the two of those are inextricably united. And therefore, there is, in that sense, an evolution of enlightenment.

"The Guru and the Pandit,"
What Is Enlightenment? no. 21: 48–49

BUT EVERY time new types of realization come into being—and that means, again, whenever the world of form has so evolved and changed that you need a different type of evolutionary enlightenment or incarnational nonduality—you've got to rewrite the instruction manual.

"The Guru and the Pandit,"
What Is Enlightenment? no. 21: 136

IT IS true that, in individuals, spirit can awaken as spirit ("spirit-as-spirit," traditional enlightenment). And it is true that this is in some important ways a *developmental* or *evolutionary* process. That is, certain developments clear the way for this timeless realization: both humans and rocks are equally spirit, but only humans can consciously realize that fact, and between the rock and the human lies evolution.

This is behind the Buddhist prayer of thanks "for this precious human body"— only in a human body can enlightenment be attained. Not gods, not animals, not demons, not angels: only with this human body can I awaken to the empty Ground that is equally present in all other sentient beings. This, too, is Aurobindo's and Murphy's emphasis on *The Future of the Body*, the precious human body. And that human body is, among many other things, the product of evolution.

And *that* means that Spirit has evolved the vehicle for its own self-realization. Because Spirit is involved with and as this world, this world evolves with and as Spirit, to the point that Spirit superconsciously realizes its own Original Face. The possibility of that realization is a product of Spirit's own evolutionary unfolding, and in that sense, this realization has a very strong developmental aspect.

But it is not the whole story. Evolution occurs in the world of time and space and form, whereas Spirit's primordial nature is finally timeless and Formless, prior to the world of evolution but not other to it. We do not find Spirit or Emptiness by reaching some evolutionary Omega point in time, but rather by stepping off the cycle of time and evolution altogether (or ceasing to contract into it).

In other words, a certain amount of evolution is required before you can step off of evolution, out of time, and into the timeless itself—into that shocking re-cognition of your own True Self, the Self that was prior to the Big Bang, prior to the temporal world altogether, eternally shining in this and every moment, untouched by the ravages of time and the motion sickness of space: your own primordial awareness is not the Omega point of the show but the Emptiness of the show, radiant in all directions, full beyond what time or space could ever do for it, yet embracing all time and all space for no other reason than that Eternity is in love with the productions of time and Infinity those of space.

Once you learn to count, you don't have to count to a million to get the point. Once you profoundly recognize Emptiness, you don't have to watch its endless displays in order to awaken. Emptiness is fully present at every point of evolution; it is not merely the end point of evolution. The game is undone in that primal Glance, and all that remains is the radiance itself, perfectly obvious in the singing of a robin, early on a bright spring dawn.

CW 7: *The Eye of Spirit*, 670–671

WE ARE part and parcel of a single and all-encompassing evolutionary current that is itself Spirit-in-action, the mode and manner of Spirit's creation, and thus is always going beyond what went before—that leaps, not crawls, to new plateaus of truth, only to leap again, dying and being reborn with each new quantum lurch, often stumbling and bruising its metaphysical knees, yet always getting right back up and jumping yet again.

And do you remember the Author of this Play? As you look deeply into your own awareness, and relax the self-contraction, and dissolve into the empty ground of your own primordial experience, the simple feeling of Being—right now, right here—is it not obvious all at once? Were you not present from the start? Did you not have a hand to play in all that was to follow? Did not the dream itself begin when you got bored with being God? Was it not fun to get lost in the productions of your own wondrous imagination, and pretend it all was other? Did you not write this book, and countless others like it, simply to remind you who you are?

CW 2: *Up from Eden*, 304

3

IMMEDIATE
AWARENESS

*It has been said that in finding the doorway to
Spirit, one must first abandon time. That is, to
recognize one's true nature means to abandon the
notions of past and future. For it is only in the
present moment that we may discover our own
Original Face.*

*From our accustomed hideouts of past and fu-
ture, of history and anticipation, Wilber flushes
us into the open space of the present moment. It is
in the naked awareness of here and now that we
become truly alive, capable of seeing ourselves
and the world directly.*

LET US begin with our senses. Do we ever
sense time? That is, do we ever directly
sense a past or a future? Start again with

hearing. For the moment concentrate your attention on just your auditory field, and notice the flux of sounds kaleidoscoping through your awareness. You might be able to hear people talking, dogs barking, kids playing; perhaps wind blowing, rain splashing, faucet dripping; maybe you can hear the house creaking, or cars honking, or someone laughing. But notice: *all* these sounds are *present* sounds. You cannot hear past sounds, nor can you hear future sounds. *The only thing you ever hear is the present.* You do not and cannot hear a past or future.

Just as all sounds are only present sounds, so all tastes are only present tastes, all smells are present smells, and all sights are present sights. You cannot touch, see, or feel anything resembling a past or a future. In other words, in your direct and immediate awareness, there is no time—no past, no future, only an endlessly changing present, shorter than a minisecond yet never coming to an end. All direct awareness is timeless awareness.

CW 1: *No Boundary*, 493

SINCE THE opposites cannot exist without each other, if you aren't aware of both of them, you will send the rejected pole underground. You will render it unconscious, and thus project it. You will, in short, create a boundary between the opposites, and thus generate a battle. But this is a battle that can never be won, only perpetually lost in way after painful way, because the two sides are actually aspects of each other.

The shadow, then, is simply your unconscious opposites. Thus, a simple way to contact your shadow is to assume the very opposite of whatever you now consciously intend, wish, or desire. That will show you exactly how your shadow looks at the world, and it is this view which you will want to befriend. This does not mean to *act* on your opposites, merely to be aware of them. If you feel you intensely dislike someone, be aware of the side of you that likes the person. If you are madly in love, be aware of the part of you that couldn't care less. If you hate a particular feeling or symptom, be aware of that aspect of yourself which secretly enjoys it. The moment you are truly aware of your opposites, of both the positive and negative feelings toward any situation, then many tensions connected with that situation drop out, because the battle of opposites which created that tension is dissolved. On the other hand, the moment you lose the unity of opposites, the awareness of both sides in yourself, then you split the opposites apart, erect a boundary between them, and thus render the rejected pole unconscious where it returns to plague you as symptom.

Since the opposites are always a unity, the only way they can be separated is by unconsciousness—selective inattention.

As you begin to explore your opposites, your shadow, your projections, you will begin to find that you are assuming responsibility for your own feelings and your own states of mind. You will start to see that most battles between you and other people are really battles between you and your projected opposites. You will start to see that your symptoms are not something that the environment is doing to you, but something you are doing to yourself as an exaggerated substitute for what you would really like to do to others. You will find that people and events don't cause you to be upset, but are merely the occasions for you to upset yourself. It is a tremendous relief when you first understand that you yourself are producing your own symptoms, because that also means you can *stop* producing those symptoms by translating them back to their original form. You become the cause of your own feelings, and not the effect.

CW 1 : *No Boundary*, 522–523

ONE OF the great discoveries of modern Western psychology is the fact that, under certain circumstances, *1st-person* impulses, feelings, and qualities can become repressed, disowned, or dissociated, and when they do, they appear as *2nd-person* or even *3rd-person* events in my own 1st-person awareness. This is one of the half-dozen truly great discoveries of all time in zone-#1 psychology, East or West, ancient or modern. . . .

To give a highly stylized example—and for this example, remember that *1st person* is defined as the person speaking (e.g., "I"); *2nd person* is the person being spoken to (e.g., "you"); and *3rd person* is the person or thing being spoken about (e.g., "him," "her," "it"). There is also "case," such as subjective, objective, and possessive case, so that, for example, *1st-person subjective* is "I," *1st-person objective* is "me," and *1st-person possessive* is "my" or "mine." So here's the stylized example of how repression or dissociation occurs:

If I become angry at my boss, but that feeling of anger is a threat to my self-sense ("I'm a nice person; nice people don't get angry"), then I might dissociate or repress the anger. But simply denying the anger doesn't get rid of it, it merely makes the angry feelings appear alien in my own awareness: I might be feeling anger, *but it is not my anger*. The angry feelings are put on the other side of the self-boundary (on the other side of the I-boundary), at which point they appear as alien or foreign events in my own awareness, in my own self.

I might, for example, project the anger. The anger continues to arise, but since it cannot be me who is angry, it must be somebody else. All of a sudden, the world appears full of people who seem to be very angry . . . , and usually at me! In fact, I think my boss wants to fire me. And this completely depresses me. Through the projection of my own anger, "mad" has become "sad." And I'm never going to get over that depression without first owning that anger.

Whenever I disown and project my own qualities, they appear "out there," where they frighten me, irritate me, depress me, obsess me. And conversely, in 9 out of 10 cases, *those things in the world that most disturb and upset me about others are actually my own shadow qualities*, which are now perceived as "out there."

Integral Spirituality, 119–120

IT IS this primal resistance to unity consciousness that we must approach, and not unity consciousness itself. For until you see precisely how you resist unity consciousness, all your efforts to "achieve" it will be in vain, because what you are trying to achieve is also what you are unconsciously resisting and trying to prevent. We secretly resist unity consciousness, we covertly manufacture the "symptoms" of nonenlightenment, just as we secretly produced all our other symptoms on the different levels of the spectrum. What on the surface we fervently desire, in the depths we successfully prevent. And this resistance is our real difficulty. Thus, we won't move *toward* unity consciousness, we will simply understand how we are always moving *away* from it. And that understanding itself might allow a glimpse of unity consciousness, *for that which sees resistance is itself free of resistance.*

CW 1: *No Boundary,* 568

MEDITATION, whether Christian, Buddhist, Hindu, Taoist, or Muslim, was invented as a way for the soul to venture inward, there ultimately to find a supreme identity with Godhead. "The Kingdom of Heaven is within"—and meditation, from the very beginning, has been the royal road to that Kingdom. Whatever else it does, and it does many beneficial things, meditation is first and foremost a search for the God within.

CW 5: *Grace and Grit*, 91

AFTER ONE has developed a strong foundation practice in vipassana, one moves on to the practice of tonglen. This practice is so powerful and so transformative it was kept largely secret until just recently in Tibet. . . . The practice is as follows:

In meditation, picture or visualize someone you know and love who is going through much suffering—an illness, a loss, depression, pain, anxiety, fear. As you breathe in, imagine all of that person's suffering—in the form of dark, black, smokelike, tarlike, thick, and heavy clouds—entering your nostrils and traveling down into your heart. Hold that suffering in your heart. Then, on the outbreath, take all of your peace, freedom, health, goodness, and virtue, and send it out to the person in the form of healing, liberating light. Imagine they take it all in, and feel completely free, released, and happy. Do that for several breaths. Then imagine the town that person is in, and, on the inbreath, take in all of the suffering of that town, and send back all of your health and happiness to everyone in it. Then do that for the entire state, then the entire country, the entire planet, the universe. You are taking in all the suffering of beings everywhere and sending them back health and happiness and virtue.

When people are first introduced to this practice, their reactions are usually strong, visceral, and negative. Mine were. Take that black tar into me? Are you kidding? What if I actually get sick? This is insane, dangerous! When Kalu [Rinpoche] first gave us these tonglen instructions, the practice of which occupied the middle portion of the retreat, a woman stood up in the audience of about one hundred people and said what virtually everybody there was thinking:

"But what if I am doing this with someone who is really sick, and I start to get that sickness myself?"

Without hesitating Kalu said, "You should think, Oh good! It's working!"

CW 5: *Grace and Grit*, 287–288

IN VIPASSANA, one simply sits in a comfortable position (lotus or half-lotus if possible, cross-legged if not), and one gives "bare attention" to whatever is arising, externally and internally, without judging it, condemning it, following after it, avoiding it, or desiring it. One simply *witnesses* it, impartially, and then lets it go. The aim of this practice is to see that the separate ego is not a real and substantial entity, but just a series of fleeting and impermanent sensations like anything else. When one realizes just how "empty" the ego is, one ceases identifying with it, defending it, worrying about it, and this in turn releases one from the chronic suffering and unhappiness that comes from defending something that isn't there. As Wei Wu Wei put it:

Why are you unhappy?
Because 99.9% of everything you think,
And everything you do,
Is for your self,
And there isn't one.

CW 5: *Grace and Grit*, 286–287

WELL, a glimmer, a taste, a hint of the non-dual—this is easy enough to catch. But for the Nondual traditions, *this is just the beginning.* As you rest in that uncontrived state of pure immediateness or pure freedom, then strange things start to happen. All of the subjective tendencies that you had previously *identified* with—all of those little selves and subjects that held open the gap between the seer and the seen—they all start burning in the freedom of nonduality. They all scream to the surface and die, and this can be a very interesting period.

As you rest in this primordial freedom of One Taste, you are no longer acting on these subjective inclinations, so they basically die of boredom, but it's still a death, and the death rattles from this liberation are very intense. You don't really have to do anything, except hold on—or let go—they're both irrelevant. It's all spontaneously accomplished by the vast expanse of primordial freedom. But you are still getting burned alive, which is just the most fun you can have without smiling.

Fundamentally, it doesn't matter what type of experience arises—the simple, natural, nondual, and uncontrived state is prior to experience, prior to duality, so it happily embraces whatever comes up. But strange things come up, and you have to stay with this "effortless effort" for quite some time, and die these little deaths constantly, and this is where real practice becomes very important.

CW 7: *A Brief History of Everything*,

264–265

AND ONCE you taste One Taste, no matter how fleetingly at first, an entirely new motivation will arise from the depths of your very own being and become a constant atmosphere which your every impulse breathes, and that atmosphere is compassion. Once you taste One Taste, and see the fundamental problems of existence evaporate in the blazing sun of obviousness, you will never again be the same person, deep within your heart. And you will want—finally, profoundly, and most of all—that others, too, may be relieved of the burden of their sleep-walking dreams, relieved of the agony of the separate self, relieved of the inherent torture called time and the gruesome tragedy called space.

No matter that lesser motivations will dog your path, no matter that anger and envy, shame and pity, pride and prejudice will remind you daily how much more you can always grow: still, and still, under it all, around it all, above it all, the heartbeat of compassion will resound. A constant cloud of caring will rain on your every parade. And you will be driven, in the best sense of the word, by this ruthless taskmaster, but only because you, eons ago, made a secret promise to let this motivation rule you until all souls are set free in the ocean of infinity.

Because of compassion, you will strive harder. Because of compassion, you will get straight. Because of compassion, you will work your fingers to the bone, push at the world until you literally bleed, toil till the tears stain your vision, struggle until life itself runs dry. And in the deepest, deepest center of your Heart, the World is already thanking you.

CW 8: *One Taste*, 579

AND TELL me: is [the] story, sung by mystics and sages the world over, any crazier than the scientific materialism story, which is that the entire sequence is a tale told by an idiot, full of sound and fury, signifying absolutely nothing? Listen very carefully:

just which of those two stories actually sounds totally insane?

I'll tell you what I think. I think the sages are the growing tip of the secret impulse of evolution. I think they are the leading edge of the self-transcending drive that always goes beyond what went before. I think they embody the very drive of the Kosmos toward greater depth and expanding consciousness. I think they are riding the edge of a light beam racing toward a rendezvous with God.

And I think they point to the same depth in you, and in me, and in all of us. I think they are plugged into the All, and the Kosmos sings through their voices, and Spirit shines through their eyes. And I think they disclose the face of tomorrow, they open us to the heart of our own destiny, which is also already right now in the timelessness of this very moment, and in that startling recognition the voice of the sage becomes your voice, the eyes of the sage become your eyes, you speak with the tongues of angels and are alight with the fire of a realization that never dawns nor ceases, you recognize your own true Face in the mirror of the Kosmos itself: your identity is indeed the All, and you are no longer *part* of that stream, you *are* that stream, with the All unfolding not around you but in you. The stars no longer shine out there, but in here. Supernovas come into being within your heart, and the sun shines inside your awareness. Because you transcend all, you embrace all. There is no final Whole here, only an endless process, and you are the opening or the clearing or the pure Emptiness in which the entire process unfolds—ceaselessly, miraculously, everlastingly, lightly.

The whole game is undone, this nightmare of evolution, and you are exactly where you were prior to the beginning of the whole show. With a sudden shock of the utterly obvious, you recognize your own Original Face, the face you had prior to the Big Bang, the face of utter Emptiness that smiles as all creation and sings as the entire Kosmos—and it is all undone in that primal glance, and all that is left is the smile, and the reflection of the moon on a quiet pond, late on a crystal clear night.

CW 7: *A Brief History of Everything*, 91

WHEN IT comes to spiritual teachers, there are those who are safe, gentle, consoling, soothing, caring; and there are the outlaws, the living terrors, the Rude Boys and Nasty Girls of God-realization, the men and women who are in your face, disturbing you, terrifying you, until you radically awaken to who and what you really are.

And may I suggest?: choose your teachers carefully.

If you want encouragement, soft smiles,

ego stroking, gentle caresses of your self-contracting ways, pats on the back and sweet words of solace, find yourself a Nice Guy or Good Girl, and hold their hand on the sweet path of stress reduction and egoic comfort. But if you want Enlightenment, if you want to wake up, if you want to get fried in the fire of passionate Infinity, then, I promise you: find yourself a Rude Boy or a Nasty Girl, the ones who make you uncomfortable in their presence, who scare you witless, who will turn on you in a second and hold you up for ridicule, who will make you wish you were never born, who will offer you not sweet comfort but abject terror, not saccharine solace but scorching angst, for then, just then, you might very well be on the path to your own Original Face. . . .

If you can stand the heat, then enter the real kitchen of your own soul, where you will find nothing other than the radiant God of the entire cosmos. For it is radiant Spirit that is looking out from your eyes right now, speaking with your tongue right now, reading the words on this very page, *right now*. Your real Self is glorious Spirit in this and every moment, and it takes a very, very Rude Boy to point that out and to stay in your face until you recognize your own Original Face, shining even here and now.

Foreword to *Living Enlightenment*
by Andrew Cohen, pp. XIII-XVIII

NOBODY WILL SAVE YOU but you. You alone have to engage your own contemplative development. There is all sorts of help available, and all sorts of good agency to quicken this development, but nobody can do it for you. And if you do not engage this development, and on your deathbed you confess and scream out for help to God, nothing is going to happen. Spiritual development is not a matter of mere belief. It is a matter of actual, prolonged difficult growth, and merely professing belief is meaningless and without impact. It's like smoking for twenty years, then saying, "Sorry, I quit." That will not impress cancer. Reality, in other words, is not interested in your beliefs; it's interested in your actions, what you actually do, your actual karma. And this is why infantile and childish views of God, once appropriate, are so detrimental for mature spirituality.

CW 4: "Paradigm Wars," 189

"THOSE WHO do in fact respond to the call of a greater tomorrow; those for whom integral culture has a deeply heartfelt ring; those in whom Spirit shines in such a way as to wish liberation for all sentient beings; those upon whom the light of the infinite is made to blaze in many hues; to whom the wind whispers tales of an all-embracing current running wildly through the Kosmos, a light that mysteriously casts no shadows in the hearts of those who see it; to all of those truly integral souls: carry your blistering vision forward, build soaring bridges where others dug moats, symphonically connect the previously unconnected, courageously pull together the ragged fragments that you find lying all around you, and we might yet live to see the day when alienation has lost its meaning, discord makes no sense, and the radiant Spirit of our own integral embrace shines freely throughout the Kosmos, announcing the home of our own awakened souls, the abode of a destiny you have always sought and finally, gloriously found."

Boomeritis, 424–425

4

PASSIONATE WORDS

In the following selections, Wilber as spiritual philosopher engages the most learned academics and enlightened sages by weaving humanity's intellectual and spiritual history into a grand integral tapestry. As a result of being inundated with technical terms from countless academic disciplines, Wilber has created a common language through which all subject areas can communicate with each other. At its best, passionate philosophy—passionate words—is not merely an intellectual transmission from one mind to another. Rather, it shakes the very core of your being.

Never does Wilber shy away from the humanity behind the thoughts—both the darkest shadows of our animal nature and the brilliant light of our divine potential. The world's collective knowledge—at all levels of depth—is included and expressed through the lens of vision-logic, which recognizes the holistic patterns and core links that fuel the integral vision. A philosophical adrenaline rush comes from discovering an utterly stunning unity within an ocean of diversity.

To HAVE any meaning at all, philosophy must sizzle with passion, boil your brain, fry your eyeballs, or you're just not doing it right. And that applies to the other end of the spectrum of feelings as well. Real philosophy is as gentle as fog and as quiet as tears; it holds the world as if it were a delicate infant, raw and open and vulnerable. I sincerely hope that if I have brought anything to this field, it is a bit of passion. . . .

The one thing I do know, and that I would like to emphasize, is that any integral theory is just that—a mere theory. I am always surprised, or rather shocked, at the common perception that I am recommending an intellectual approach to spirituality, when that is the opposite of my view. Just because an author writes, say, a history of dancing, does not mean that the author is advocating that people stop dancing and merely read about it instead. I have written academic treatises that cover areas such as spirituality and its relation to a larger scheme of things, but my recommendation is always that people take up an actual spiritual practice, rather than merely read about it. An integral approach to dancing says, take up dancing itself, and sure, read a book about it, too. Do both, but in any event, don't merely read the book. That's like taking a vacation to Bermuda by sitting at home and looking through a book of maps. My books are maps, but please, go to Bermuda and see for yourself.

Foreword to *Ken Wilber: Thought as Passion* by Frank Visser, pp. XII–XIV

MEN AND WOMEN, as the Christian mystics are fond of saying, have (at least) three eyes of knowing: the eye of flesh, which apprehends physical events; the eye of mind, which apprehends images and desires and concepts and ideas; and the eye of contemplation, which apprehends spiritual experiences and states. And that, of course, is a simplified version of the spectrum of consciousness, reaching from body to mind to spirit.

CW 7: *The Eye of Spirit*, 447

THE ULTIMATE metaphysical secret, if we dare state it so simply, is that there are no boundaries in the universe. Boundaries are illusions, products not of reality but of the way we map and edit reality. And while it is fine to map out the territory, it is fatal to confuse the two.

CW 1: *No Boundary*, 462

WHAT ONE is attempting to "destroy" in contemplation *is not the mind but an exclusive identity of consciousness with the mind.*

CW 3: *A Sociable God,* 107

Q: Do you think the "final paradigm" is actually "final"? Do you think this realization, the realization of the sages, do you think that this is unchanging and forever invariant?

KW: No, not like that. Hegel actually went from thinking that "enlightenment" was an end state, a final product, to seeing it as an eternal process. The great Japanese meditation master, Dogen Zenji, had probably the greatest line ever on spiritual development. It manages to pack virtually everything you can say about spiritual development into four lines. Dogen said, "To study Buddhism"—but I'm going to take the liberty of changing the word "Buddhism" to "mysticism," because that is what it really refers to—"To study mysticism is to study the self. To study the self is to forget the self. To forget the self is to be one with all things. To be one with all things is to be enlightened by all things, and this traceless enlightenment continues forever."

In other words, enlightenment is a process, not an end state, not a product. It goes on forever. . . . "And this traceless enlightenment continues forever. . . ." That is the testimony, the confession of the world's great sages. And in that sense, and that sense only, you have the final paradigm, which continues forever as a process. . . . And it does not involve some sort of New Age hoopla and narcissism and me-ness and oh-boy. It involves "wu-shih" . . . nobody special. Nobody special . . . you see?

CW 4: "Paradigm Wars," 194–195

THE MYSTICAL experience is indeed ineffable, or not capable of being entirely put into words; like any experience—a sunset, eating a piece of cake, listening to Bach's music—one has to have the actual experience to see what it's like. We don't conclude, however, that sunset, cake, and music therefore don't exist or aren't valid. Further, even though the mystical experience is largely ineffable, it *can* be communicated or transmitted, namely, by taking up spiritual practice under the guidance of a spiritual master or teacher (much as judo can be taught but not spoken; as Wittgenstein would have it, the mystical "can be shown but not said").

CW 4: "Two Humanistic Psychologies?," 227

PHILOSOPHICALLY, we are going to have to face and acknowledge the fact that rational-mental statements about Spirit or

Being always eventually degenerate in contradictions or paradoxes.

CW 3: *Eye to Eye*, 221

EVERY FORM of meditation is basically a way to transcend the ego, or die to the ego. In that sense, meditation mimics death—that is, death of the ego. If one progresses fairly well in *any* meditation system, one eventually comes to a point of having so exhaustively "witnessed" the mind and body that one actually rises above, or transcends, the mind and body, thus "dying" to them, to the ego, and awakening as subtle soul or even spirit. And this is actually experienced as a death. In Zen it is called the Great Death. It can be a fairly easy experience, a relatively peaceful transcendence of subject-object dualism, or—because it is a real death of sorts—it can also be terrifying. But subtly or dramatically, quickly or slowly, the sense of being a separate self dies, or is dissolved, and one finds a prior and higher identity in and as universal spirit.

CW 4: "Death, Rebirth, and Meditation," 352

SATORI IS a "direct seeing into one's nature"—as perfectly direct as looking into the microscope to see the cell nucleus, with the important proviso in each case: only a trained eye need look.

CW 3: *A Sociable God*, 129

THE ANSWER to the relation of the Absolute and the relative is therefore most definitely *not*: the Absolute created the world. It most definitely is *not*: the world is illusory and the Absolute alone is real. It is *not*: we perceive only the phenomenal reflection of a noumenal reality. It is *not*: fate and free will are two aspects of one and the same process. It is *not*: all things and events are different aspects of a single interwoven web-of-life. It is *not*: the body alone is real and the mind is a reflection of that only reality. It is *not*: mind and body are two different aspects of the total organism. It is *not*: mind emerges from hierarchical brain structure. In fact, it is not even: noumenon and phenomena are not-two and nondual.

Those are all merely *intellectual symbols* that purport to give the answer, but the real answer does not lie in sensibilia or intelligibilia, it lies in transcendelia, and that domain only discloses itself after the meditative exemplar is engaged, whereupon every single one of those intellectual answers is seen to be inadequate and off the mark; each generates nothing but more insolvable and insuperable difficulties, dilemmas, and contradictions. The answer is not more talk; the answer is satori, by whatever name we wish to use to convey valid contemplative awareness.

And, much more to the point, even if this answer could be stated in words—and in fact, the answer can be stated in words, because Zen masters talk about it all the time!—nonetheless, it would make no sense to anybody who had not also performed the injunction, just as mathematical symbols can be seen by anybody but understood only by those who have completed the training.

But open the eye of contemplation, and the answer is as obvious, as perfect, as unmistakable as the play of sunlight on a crystal clear pond, early on a cool spring morning.

You see, that was the answer.

CW 7: *The Eye of Spirit*, 501

WHAT IS important is not my particular version of an integral view, but rather that we all begin to enter into this extraordinary dialogue about the possibility of an integral approach in general, an approach that—we can say this in several different ways—integrates the hard-headed with the soft-hearted, the natural sciences with the noetic sciences, objective realities with subjective realities, the empirical with the transcendental.

And so let us hope that a decade from now somebody might spot a great mega-trend in consciousness studies—namely, the truly integral—and let it start right now with all of us who share this concern for holism, for embrace, for synthesizing, for integrating: let this outreach start with us, right here, right now.

CW 8: *One Taste*, 376

THE TOTALITY of all manifestation at any time—the All—subsists in the low causal, as the sum total of the consequent and primordial nature of Spirit (in roughly Whitehead's sense), and this Totality is the *manifest* omega pull on each individual and finite thing: as such, it is ever-receding: each new moment has a new total horizon that can never be reached or fulfilled, because the moment of fulfillment itself creates a new whole of which the previous whole is now a part: cascading whole/parts all the way up, holons endlessly self-transcending and thus never finally self-fulfilled: rushing forward ceaselessly in time attempting to find the timeless.

And the *final* Omega, the *ultimate* and *unmanifest* Omega, the causal Formless, is the magnet *on the other side* of the horizon, which never itself enters the world of Form as a singularity or as a totality (or any other phenomenal event), and thus is never found at all in any version of manifestation, even though all manifestation will rest nowhere short of this infinite Emptiness.

Thus, from any angle, there is no ultimate Omega to be found in the world of Form. There is no Perfection in the manifest world. Were the world of Form to find Perfection and utter fulfillment, there would be nothing else for it to do and nowhere else for it to go: nothing further to want, to desire, to seek, to find: the entire world would cease its search, stop its drive, end its very movement: would become without motion, time, or space: would become the Formless. But the Formless is already there, on the other side of the horizon, which is to say, the Formless is already there as the deepest depth of this and every moment.

This Deepest Depth is the desire of all Form, which cannot itself be reached in the world of Form, but rather is the Emptiness of each and every Form: when all Forms are seen to be always already Formless, then dawns the Nondual empty Ground that is the Suchness and the Thusness of each and every display. The entire world of Form is always already Perfectly Empty, always already in the ever-present Condition of all conditions, always already the ultimate Omega that is not the goal of each and every thing but the Suchness of each and every thing: *just this*. The search is always already over, and Forms continue their eternal play as a gesture of the Divine, not seeking Spirit but expressing Spirit in their every move and motion.

CW 6: *Sex, Ecology, Spirituality*, 655

AND WHERE the moons of Jupiter can be disclosed by the eye of flesh or its extensions (sensory data), and the Pythagorean theorem can be disclosed by the eye of mind and its inward apprehensions (mental data), the nature of Spirit can be disclosed only by the *eye of contemplation* and its directly disclosed referents: the direct experiences, apprehensions, and data of the spiritual domain.

CW 8: *The Marriage of Sense and Soul*, 230

GENUINE SPIRITUALITY, we will see, is primarily a measure of depth and a disclosure of depth. There is *more* spirituality in reason's *denial* of God than there is in myth's *affirmation* of God, precisely because there is *more depth*. (And the transrational, in turn, discloses yet more depth, yet more Spirit, than either myth or reason).

But the very *depth* of reason, its capacity for universal-pluralism, its insistence on universal tolerance, its grasp of global-planetary perspectivism, its insistence on universal benevolence and compassion: these are the manifestations of its genuine depth, its *genuine* spirituality. These capacities are not *revealed* to reason from *without* (by a mythic source); they issue from *within* its own structure, its own *inherent* depth (which is why it does not need recourse to a mythic god to implement its agenda of universal benevolence, why even an "atheist" acting from rational-universal compassion is more spiritual than a fundamentalist acting to convert the universe in the name of a mythic-membership god). That the Spirit of reason does not fly through the sky hurling thunderbolts and otherwise spend its time turning spinach into potatoes speaks more, not less, on its behalf.

CW 6: *Sex, Ecology, Spirituality*, 259

IN THIS Theory of Everything, I have one major rule: *Everybody* is right. More specifically, everybody—including me—has some important pieces of truth, and all of those pieces need to be honored, cherished, and included in a more gracious, spacious, and compassionate embrace. . . .

A Theory of Everything, 140

[THE TEACHINGS of the world's greatest yogis, saints, and sages,] and their contemplative endeavors, were (and are) transrational through and through. That is, although all of the contemplative traditions aim at going within and beyond reason, they all *start* with reason, start with the notion that truth is to be established by *evidence*, that truth is the result of *experimental* methods, that truth is to be *tested* in the laboratory of personal *experience*, that these truths are open to all those who wish to *try the experiment* and thus disclose *for themselves* the truth or falsity of the spiritual claims—and that dogmas or given beliefs are precisely what hinder the emergence of deeper truths and wider visions.

Thus, each of these spiritual or transpersonal endeavors (which we will carefully examine) claims that there exist higher domains of awareness, embrace, love, identity, reality, self, and truth. But these claims are not dogmatic; they are not believed in merely because an authority proclaimed them, or because sociocentric tradition hands them down, or because salvation depends upon being a "true believer." Rather, the claims about these higher domains are a *conclusion* based on hundreds of years of experimental introspection and communal verification. False claims are *rejected* on the basis of *consensual evidence*, and further evidence is used to adjust and fine-tune the experimental conclusions.

These spiritual endeavors, in other words, are scientific in any meaningful sense of the word, and the systematic presentations of these endeavors follow precisely those of any *reconstructive science*.

CW 6: *Sex, Ecology, Spirituality*, 273

WHETHER, IN the end, you believe spiritual practice involves stages or not, authentic spirituality does involve *practice*. This is not to deny that for many people beliefs are important, faith is important, religious mythology is important. It is simply to add that, as the testimony of the world's great yogis, saints, and sages has made quite clear, authentic spirituality can also involve direct *experience* of a living Reality, disclosed immediately and intimately in the heart and consciousness of individuals, and fostered by diligent, sincere, prolonged spiritual practice. Even if you relate to spirituality as a peak experience, those peak experiences can often be specifically induced, or at least invited, by various forms of spiritual practice, such as active ritual, contemplative prayer, shamanic voyage, intensive meditation, and so forth. All of those open one to a direct experience of Spirit, and not merely beliefs or ideas about Spirit.

Therefore, don't just think differently, practice diligently.

CW 4: *Integral Psychology*, 568

WHEN YOU practice meditation, one of the first things you realize is that your mind—and your life, for that matter—is dominated by largely subconscious verbal chatter. You are always talking to yourself. And so, as they start to meditate, many people are stunned by how much junk starts running through their awareness. They find that thoughts, images, fantasies, notions, ideas, concepts virtually dominate their awareness. They realize that these notions have had a much more profound influence on their lives than they ever thought.

In any case, initial meditation experiences are like being at the movies. You sit and watch all these fantasies and concepts parade by, in front of your awareness. But the whole point is that you are finally becoming aware of them. You are looking at them impartially and without judgment. You just watch them go by, the same as you watch clouds float by in the sky. They come, they go. No praise, no condemnation, no judgment—just "bare witnessing." If you judge your thoughts, if you get caught up in them, then you can't transcend them. You can't find higher or subtler dimensions of your own being. So you sit in meditation, and you simply "witness" what is going on in your mind. You let the monkey mind do what it wants, and you simply watch.

And what happens is, because you impartially witness these thoughts, fantasies, notions, and images, you start to become free of their unconscious influence. You are looking at them, so you are not using them to look at the world. Therefore you become, to a certain extent, free of them. And you become free of the separate-self sense that depended on them. In other words, you start to become free of the ego. This is the initial spiritual dimension, where the conventional ego "dies" and higher structures of awareness are "resurrected." Your sense of identity naturally begins to expand and embrace the cosmos, or all of nature. You rise above the isolated mind and body, which might include finding a larger identity, such as with nature or the cosmos— "cosmic consciousness," as R. M. Bucke called it. It's a very concrete and unmistakable experience.

CW 4: "Stages of Meditation," 357–358

SAY YOU are walking downtown, looking in shop windows. You're looking at some of the merchandise, and all of a sudden you see a vague image dance in front of your eyes, the image of a person. Then all at once you realize that it is your own reflection in the shop window. You suddenly recognize yourself. You recognize your Self, your higher Self. You suddenly recognize who you are. And who you are is—a luminous spark of the Divine. But it has that shock of recognition—"Oh, that!"

CW 4: "Stages of Meditation," 359–360

THERE ARE several different ways that we can state . . . two important functions of religion. The first function—that of creating meaning for the self—is a type of *horizontal* movement; the second function—that of transcending the self—is a type of *vertical* movement (higher or deeper, depending on your metaphor). The first I have named *translation*; the second, *transformation*.

With translation, the self is simply given a new way to think or feel about reality. The self is given a new belief—perhaps holistic instead of atomistic, perhaps forgiveness instead of blame, perhaps relational instead of analytic. The self then learns to translate its world and its being in the terms of this new belief or new language or new paradigm, and this new and enchanting translation acts, at least temporarily, to alleviate or diminish the terror inherent in the heart of the separate self.

But with transformation, the very process of translation itself is challenged, witnessed, undermined, and eventually dismantled. With typical *translation*, the self (or subject) is given a new way to think about the world (or objects); but with radical *transformation*, the self itself is inquired into, looked into, grabbed by its throat and

THE POCKET KEN WILBER

literally throttled to death. . . . The self is not made content; the self is made toast.

CW 8: *One Taste*, 304–305

AUTHENTIC SPIRITUALITY, in short, must be based on direct spiritual experience, and this must be rigorously subjected to the three strands of valid knowledge: injunction, apprehension, and confirmation/rejection—or exemplar, data, and falsifiability. . . .

It is only when religion emphasizes its heart and soul and essence—namely, direct mystical experience and transcendental consciousness, which is disclosed not by the eye of flesh (give that to science) nor by the eye of mind (give that to philosophy) but rather by the eye of contemplation—that religion can both stand up to modernity and offer something for which modernity has desperate need: a genuine, verifiable, repeatable injunction to bring forth the spiritual domain.

CW 8: *The Marriage of Sense and Soul*, 227

EARLY MORNING, the orange sun is slowly rising, shining forth in empty luminous clarity. The mind and the sky are one, the sun is rising in the vast space of primordial awareness, and there is *just this*. Yasutani Roshi once said, speaking of satori, that it was the most precious realization in the world, because all the great philosophers had tried to understand ultimate reality but had failed to do so, yet with satori or awakening all of your deepest questions are finally answered: it's *just this*.

CW 8: *One Taste*, 383

THUS ULTIMATELY Emptiness takes no sides in a conceptual argument; Emptiness is not a view that can dislodge other views; it cannot be brought in to support one view as opposed to another: it is the Emptiness of all views, period.

CW 6: *Sex, Ecology, Spirituality*, 7 2 4

WHEN ALL is said and done, and argument and theory come to rest, and the separate self lays its weary head on the pillow of its own discontent, what then? When I relax into I-I, and the infinite spaciousness of primordial purity drenches me in Being; when I relax into I-I, and the eternal Emptiness of ever-present awareness saturates the self, fills it with a Fullness that cannot even be contained; then all the agitated anxieties of life return to their source in God and Goddess, and I-I alone shine in the world that I-I alone created. Where is suffering then?, and how do you even pronounce misery? There in the Heart, where the mathematics of torture and the physics of pain can find no purchase or way to disturb, then all things bright and beautiful come out to dance in the day's glorious sun, long forgotten by the contracting ways of the loveless and forlorn self, god of its own perception, engineer of its own agony.

It is, truly, a game; what dream walkers we all are! Nothing ever really happens here, nothing moves in time or space, it is all so painfully obvious that I avert my eyes from the blinding truth. But here we are, You and I, and it is You-and-I that is the form of Spirit in this and all the worlds. For in the entire Kosmos, there is only One Self; in the entire Kosmos, there is only One Spirit—and thus the Self that is reading this page is exactly the Self that wrote it.

Let us, then, You-and-I, recognize together who and what we are. And I will be with you until the ends of the world, and you will be with me, for there is only One

Self, which is the miracle of Spirit. This is why we will be together forever, You-and-I, in the world of the Many-That-Are-One, and why we have never been separated. Just as Consciousness is singular, and the Self is One, and the Self neither comes nor goes, so You-and-I are that Self, forever and forever and endlessly forever.

Thank you deeply for coming on this journey with me, and guiding me at every point, and enlightening me through and through, and forgiving me all along, and being You-and-I.

CW 8: *Introduction*, 49–50

5

BEING-IN-
THE-WORLD

*It is not enough to ascend into the heights of
Heaven if you are not to the same degree engaged
with the manifestations of this world. Likewise,
an embrace of this world becomes even more spiritual insofar as it discovers Pure Space in the
folds of earthly life. In this chapter, Wilber's
writings highlight how the Divine manifests in
and through the everyday world of our lives and
our communities.*

*Wilber issues a clarion call to liberate all
perspectives into an integral chorus of inclusion-
in-diversity. He invites everyone to be Spirit in
this world, to be in compassionate relationship
with all beings and their perspectives, and to be
able to take on viewpoints that differ from or*

contradict one's own. All individuals are embedded in communities of understanding, which create various horizons of meaning. The interplay of these horizons of meaning is what gives the global village such a dynamic potential and why an integral understanding of Being-in-the-World is so essential.

So THE whole point, I think, is that we want to find ourselves in sympathetic attunement with all aspects of the Kosmos. We want to find ourselves at home in the Kosmos. We want to touch the truth in [all domains]. We begin to do so by noticing that each speaks to us with a different voice. If we listen carefully, we can hear each of these voices whispering gently their truths, and finally joining in a harmonious chorus that quietly calls us home. We can fully resonate with those liberating truths, if we know how to recognize and honor them.

From attunement to atonement to at-onement: we find ourselves in the over-powering embrace of a Kosmic sympathy on the very verge of Kosmic consciousness itself . . . if we listen very carefully.

CW 7: *A Brief History of Everything*, 147

It is often said that in today's modern and postmodern world, the forces of darkness are upon us. But I think not; in the Dark and the Deep there are truths that can always heal. It is not the forces of darkness but of shallowness that everywhere threaten the true, and the good, and the beautiful, and that ironically announce themselves as deep and profound. It is an exuberant and fear-less shallowness that everywhere is the modern danger, the modern threat, and that everywhere nonetheless calls to us as savior.

We might have lost the Light and the

Height; but more frightening, we have lost the Mystery and the Deep, the Emptiness and the Abyss, and lost it in a world dedicated to surfaces and shadows, exteriors and shells, whose prophets lovingly exhort us to dive into the shallow end of the pool head first.

"History," said Emerson, "is an impertinence and an injury if it be anything more than a cheerful apologue or parable of my being and becoming." What follows, then, is a cheerful parable of your being and your becoming, an apologue of that Emptiness which forever issues forth, unfolding and enfolding, evolving and involving, creating worlds and dissolving them, with each and every breath you take. This is a chronicle of what you have done, a tale of what you have seen, a measure of what we all might yet become.

CW 6: *Sex, Ecology, Spirituality*, 7

WHAT DOES a "space" or "clearing" mean in this regard? Originating with Heidegger, but taking on numerous other (yet related) meanings, the idea is essentially this: reality is not a pregiven monological entity lying around for all to see; rather, various social practices and cultural contexts create an opening or clearing in which various types of subjects and objects can appear. For example, as I would put it, the magic world-space creates a clearing in which animistic objects can appear; the mythic worldspace creates a space in which a caring God can appear; the rational worldspace creates a clearing in which worldcentric compassion can appear; the psychic worldspace creates a space in which the World Soul can appear; the causal worldspace creates a clearing in which the Abyss can be recognized. None of those are simply lying around out there and hitting the eyeballs of everybody. There is no single "pregiven world" (*the* essential insight of postmodernism).

CW 6: *Sex, Ecology, Spirituality*, 775

BY UNDERSTANDING [the variety of] different truths, and acknowledging them, we can more sympathetically include them in an integral embrace. We can more expansively attune ourselves to the Kosmos. The final result might even be an attunement with the All, might even be Kosmic consciousness itself. Why not? But I think first we need to understand these various truths, so they can begin to speak to us, in us, through us—and we can begin to hear their voices and honor them, and thus invite all of them together into a rainbow coalition, an integral embrace.

These truths are behind much of the great postmodern rebellion. They are the key to the interior and transcendental dimensions; they speak eloquently in tongues of hidden gods and angels; they point to the heart of holons in general, and invite us into that interior world; they are antidote to the flat and faded world that passes for today. We might even say that [the] four types of truth [the interiors and exteriors of individuals and collectives] are the four faces of Spirit as it shines in the manifest world.

CW 7: *A Brief History of Everything*, 1 2 8

So MY supposedly "individual thought" is actually a phenomenon that intrinsically has (at least) . . . four aspects to it—intentional, behavioral, cultural, and social. And around the holistic circle we go: the social system will have a strong influence on the cultural worldview, which will set limits to the individual thoughts that I can have, which will register in the brain physiology. And we can go around that circle in any direction. They are all interwoven. They are all mutually determining. They all cause, and are caused by, the others, in concentric spheres of contexts within contexts indefinitely.

CW 7: *The Eye of Spirit*, 429

THE PRIME directive asks us to honor and appreciate the necessary, vital, and unique contribution provided by each and every wave of consciousness unfolding, and thus act to *protect and promote the health of the entire spiral*, and not any one privileged domain. At the same time, it invites us to offer, as a gentle suggestion, a conception of a more complete spectrum of consciousness, a full spiral of development, so that individuals or cultures (including ours) that are not aware of some of the deeper or higher dimensions of human possibilities may choose to act on those extraordinary resources, which in turn might help to defuse some of the recalcitrant problems that have not yielded to less integral approaches.

A Theory of Everything, 102–103

I AM often asked, why even attempt an integration of the various worldviews? Isn't it enough to simply celebrate the rich diversity of various views and not try to integrate them? Well, recognizing diversity is certainly a noble endeavor, and I heartily support that pluralism. But if we remain merely at the stage of celebrating diversity, we ultimately are promoting fragmentation, alienation, separation and despair. You go your way, I go my way, we both fly apart—which is often what has happened under the reign of the pluralistic relativists, who have left us a postmodern Tower of Babel on too many fronts. It is not enough to recognize the many ways in which we are all different; we need to go further and start recognizing the many ways that we are also similar. Otherwise we simply contribute to heapism, not wholism. Building on the rich diversity offered by pluralistic relativism, we need to take the next step and weave those many strands into a holonic spiral of unifying connections, an interwoven Kosmos of mutual intermeshing. We need, in short, to move from pluralistic relativism to universal integralism—we need to keep trying to find the One-in-the-Many that is the form of the Kosmos itself.

A Theory of Everything, 112

•

FINDING GOD through sex? And why not? The only thing that is astonishing in that equation is that it ever should have seemed odd to begin with. For many of the world's great wisdom traditions, particularly in their mature phases, sexuality was deeply viewed as an exquisite expression of spirituality—and a path to further spiritual realization. After all, in the ecstatic embrace of sexual love, we are taken far beyond ourselves, released from the cramp of the separate self, delivered at least temporarily into timeless, spaceless, blissful union with the wondrous beloved: and what better definition of spiritual release is there than that? We all taste God, taste Goddess, taste pure Spirit in those moments of sexual rapture, and wise men and women have always used that rapture to reveal Spirit's innermost secrets.

Foreword to *Finding God Through Sex*
by David Deida, IX

LOVE FOR a specific person is radiant when it arises in Emptiness. It is still love, it is still intensely personal, it is still very specific;

but it is a wave that arises from an ocean of infinity. It is as if a great sea of love brings forth a wave, and that wave carries the force and thrill of the entire sea in its every breaking crest. The sensation is like watching an early morning sunrise in the desert: a vast open clear blue spaciousness, within which there arises, on the horizon, an intense red-yellow fire. You are the infinite sky of Love, in which a particular fire-ball of personal love arises.

One thing is certain: infinite love and personal love are not mutually exclusive—the latter is just an individual wave of an infinite ocean. When I lie awake, next to her, early in the morning, doing meditation, nothing really changes in the contemplation except this: there is a whole-body bliss, paradoxically faint but intense, that edges my awareness. It is sexual energy reconnected to its source in the subtle regions of the bodymind. I will often touch her lightly as I meditate; it definitely completes an energy circuit, and she can feel it, too.

But that is what men and women (as well as "butch/femme" pairings across sexual orientations) can do for each other, and that is the core claim of Tantra as well: in a very concrete, visceral way, the union of male and female is the union of Eros and Agape, Ascending and Descending, Emptiness and Form, Wisdom and Compassion. Not theoretically but concretely, in the actual distribution of prana or energy currents in the body itself. And this is why, in the very highest Tantric teachings (anuttaratantrayoga), the mere visualization of sexual congress with the divine consort is not enough for final enlightenment. Rather, for ultimate enlightenment, one must take an actual partner—real sex—in order to complete the circuits conducive to recognizing the already-enlightened mind.

CW 8: One Taste, 461

THE GENERAL idea of integral practice [or Integral Life Practice] is clear enough: *Exercise body, mind, soul, and spirit in self, culture, and nature. . . .* Pick a basic practice from each category, or from as many categories as pragmatically possible, and practice them concurrently. The more categories engaged, the more effective they all become (because they are all intimately related as aspects of your own being). Practice them diligently, and coordinate your integral efforts to unfold the various potentials of the bodymind—until the bodymind itself unfolds in Emptiness, and the entire journey is a misty memory from a trip that never even occurred.

CW 4: *Integral Psychology*, 546

I WOULD like to propose the thesis that the Basic Moral Intuition (BMI)—present at all stages of human growth—is "Protect and promote the greatest depth for the greatest span." This BMI represents (*is a direct result of*) the manifestation of Spirit in the four quadrants (or simply the Big Three)—the depth in I expanded to include others (we) in a corresponding objective state of affairs (it). That is, all individuals intuit Spirit, and since Spirit *manifests* as the Big Three, then the basic spiritual intuition is felt in all three domains, and thus the basic spiritual intuition ("Honor and actualize Spirit") shows up as "Promote the greatest depth for the greatest span," or so I maintain.*

CW 6: *Sex, Ecology, Spirituality*, 640–641

TRANSCENDENCE RESTORES humor. Spirit brings smiling. Suddenly, laughter returns. Too many representatives of too

---

* For a summary of the four quadrants, see the introduction to *The Eye of the Spirit*, CW 7, 429–450.

many movements—even very good movements, such as feminism, ecology, and spiritual studies—seem to lack humor altogether. In other words, they lack lightness, they lack a distance from themselves, a distance from the ego and its grim game of forcing others to conform to its contours. There is self-transcending humor, or there is the game of egoic power. But we have chosen egoic power and politically correct thought police; grim Victorian reformers pretending to be defending civil rights; messianic new-paradigm thinkers who are going to save the planet and heal the world. No wonder Mencken wrote that "Every third American devotes himself to improving and lifting up his fellow citizens, usually by force; this messianic delusion is our national disease." Perhaps we should all trade two pounds of ego for one ounce of laughter.

CW 8: *One Taste*, 582

FOR THE real intent of my writing is not to say, You must think in this way. The real intent is: here are some of the many important facets of this extraordinary Kosmos; have you thought about including them in your own worldview? My work is an attempt to make room in the Kosmos for all of the dimensions, levels, domains, waves, memes, modes, individuals, cultures, and so on ad infinitum. I have one major rule: *everybody* is right. More specifically, everybody—including me—has some important pieces of truth, and all of those pieces need to be honored, cherished, and included in a more gracious, spacious, and compassionate embrace. To Freudians I say, Have you looked at Buddhism? To Buddhists I say, Have you studied Freud? To liberals I say, Have you thought about how important some conservative ideas are? To conservatives I say, Can you perhaps include a more liberal perspective? And so on, and so on, and so on. . . . At no point have I ever said: Freud is wrong, Buddha is wrong, liberals are wrong, conservatives are wrong. I have only suggested that they are true but partial. My critical writings have never attacked the central beliefs of any discipline, only the claims that the particular discipline has the only truth—and on those grounds I have often been harsh. But every approach, I honestly believe, is essentially true but partial, true but partial, true but partial.

And on my own tombstone, I dearly hope that someday they will write: He was true but partial. . . .

CW 8: *Introduction*, 49

"THE TYPICAL New Age notion is that you want good things to happen to you, so think good thoughts; and because you create your own reality, those thoughts will come true. Conversely, if you are sick, it's because you have been bad. The mystical notion, on the other hand, is that your deepest Self transcends *both* good and bad, so by accepting *absolutely everything* that happens to you—by equally embracing both good and bad *with equanimity*—you can transcend the ego altogether. The idea is *not* to have one thing that is good smash into another thing called my ego, but to gently rise above both."

Boomeritis, 336

"You CAN be God, or you can be an ego pretending to be God. It's your choice."

Boomeritis, 376

To SEE our resistance to unity consciousness is to be able, for the first time, to deal with it and finally to drop it—thus removing the secret obstacle to our own liberation.

CW 1: *No Boundary*, 566

ALL LESSER stages, no matter how occasionally ecstatic or visionary, are still beset with the primal mood of ego, which is sickness unto death. Even the saint, according to the sages, has yet to finally surrender his or her soul, or separate-self sense, and this prevents the saint from attaining absolute identity with and as Godhead.

CW 3: *A Sociable God*, 66

WHEN SPIRIT is de-mythologized, it can be approached *as* Spirit, in its Absolute Suchness (*tathata*), and not as a cosmic Parent.

CW 3: *A Sociable God*, 87

THE SECRET of all genuinely spiritual works of art is that they issue from nondual or unity consciousness, no matter what "objects" they portray. . . . The artwork, no matter what the object, becomes transparent to the Divine, and is a direct expression of Spirit.

The viewer momentarily *becomes* the art and is for that moment released from the alienation that is ego. Great spiritual art dissolves ego into nondual consciousness, and is to that extent experienced as an epiphany; a revelation, release or liberation from the tyranny of the separate-self sense. To the extent that a work can usher one into the nondual, then it is spiritual or universal, no matter whether it depicts bugs or Buddhas.

CW 4: "In the Eye of the Artist," Foreword to *Sacred Mirrors: The Visionary Art of Alex Grey*, 379

THE SELF doesn't live forever in time, it lives in the timeless present prior to time, prior to history, change, succession. The Self is present as Pure Presence, not as everlasting duration, a rather horrible notion.

CW 5: *Grace and Grit*, 103

DIFFERENT MEDITATION practices engineer different states and different experiences, but pure Presence itself is unwavering, and thus the highest approach in Dzogchen is "Buddhahood without meditation": not the creation but the *direct recognition* of an already perfectly present and freely given primordial Purity, of the pure Emptiness of this and every state, embracing equally all forms: embracing a self, embracing a no-self, embracing whatever arises....

And yet, and yet: how best to refer to

this always already Emptiness? What words could a fish use to refer to water? How could you point out water to a fish? Drenched in it, never apart from it, upheld by it—what are we to do? Splash water in its face? What if its original face *is* water?

CW 6: *Sex, Ecology, Spirituality*, 730–731

6

ALWAYS ALREADY

Prior to form is formless Emptiness, and formless Emptiness is saturated with form. This is the play of the Kosmos, that which is always already simply Spirit. While myriad expressions of form unceasingly arise and pass away each instant, beyond time and space is the eternal now, the ever-present moment. This timeless eternity is always available to us, as if waiting to be recalled. It is through this sacred act of remembrance that we may come to know that which was never born and will never die.

Through momentary suspensions of our will, gaps in the implacable churning of our ego, we can touch the eternal Absolute Spirit that precedes the manifest world, that which is known as One Taste. The following selections at once open such gaps and usher us through them into the re-

*alization of One Taste that we already have, and
always have had.*

This morning, only vast Emptiness.
I-I is only, alone with the Alone, all in
  All.
Fullness pushes me out of existence,
Radiance blinds me to the things of this
  world,
I see only infinite Freedom,
which means I see nothing at all.
There is a struggle to reanimate the soul,
to crank consciousness down and into
  the subtle,
to pull it down into ego and body,
and thus get out of bed at all.
But the Freedom is still there,
in this little twilight dawn,
and Release inhabits even
the smallest moves to make manifest
this glorious Estate.

CW 8: *One Taste*, 391

Do you recognize the Timeless One, even here and now, that is spontaneously aware of all of this? If so, please tell me, Who and What are you, when you are deeper than within? Clouds pass by, feelings pass by, thoughts pass by—but what in you does not pass by? Do you see That One? Can you say its Name?

Boomeritis, 121

THE DESIRES of the flesh, the ideas of the mind, and the luminosities of the soul—all are perfect expressions of the radiant Spirit that alone inhabits the universe, sublime gestures of that Great Perfection that alone outshines the world. There is only One Taste in the entire Kosmos, and that taste is Divine, whether it appears in the flesh, in the mind, in the soul. Resting in that One Taste, transported beyond the mundane, the world arises in the purest Freedom and radiant Release, happy to infinity, lost in all eternity, and hopeless in the original face of the unrelenting mystery. From One Taste all things issue, to One Taste all things return—and in between, which is the story of this moment, there is only the dream, and sometimes the nightmare, from which we would do well to awaken.

CW 8: *One Taste*, 278

THE ESSENCE of mysticism is that in the deepest part of your own being, in the very center of your own pure awareness, you are fundamentally one with Spirit, one with Godhead, one with the All, in a timeless and eternal and unchanging fashion.

CW 5: *Grace and Grit*, 22

THUS, WHETHER we realize it or not, want it or not, care about it or not, understand it or not, we are It—always have been and always will be. . . .

Now because we are It, we can never attain It, get It, reach It, grab It, or find It, any more than we can run after our own feet. In a sense, then, all search for Mind is ultimately in vain. . . .

As a matter of fact, just because we are It, any search for It not only "is doomed to failure" but actually creates the impression that we lack It! By our very seeking, we apparently drive It away, just as if we misguidedly started looking for our head it would imply that we had lost it.

CW 1: *The Spectrum of Consciousness*,
329–330

AROUND THE sea of Emptiness, a faint
    edge of bliss.
From the sea of Emptiness, a flicker of
    compassion.

Subtle illuminations fill the space of
    awareness,
As radiant forms coalesce in
    consciousness.
A world is taking shape,
A universe is being born.
I-I breathe out the subtlest patterns,
Which crystallize into the densest
    forms,
With physical colors, things, objects,
    processes,
That rush upon awareness in the
    darkness of its night,
To arise as glorious sun, radiant
    reminder of its source,
And slumbering earth, abode of the
    offspring of Spirit.

CW 8: *One Taste*, 419

IN THE stillness of the night, the Goddess
whispers. In the brightness of the day, dear

God roars. Life pulses, mind imagines, emotions wave, thoughts wander. What are these but the endless movements of One Taste, forever at play with its own gestures, whispering quietly to all who would listen: is this not you yourself? When the thunder roars, do you not hear your Self? When the lightning cracks, do you not see your Self? When clouds float quietly across the sky, is this not your very own limitless Being, waving back at you?

CW 8: *One Taste*, 557–558

CLEARLY, in this present moment, if we would but examine it, there is no time. The present moment is a timeless moment, and a timeless moment is an eternal one—a moment which knows neither past nor future, before nor after, yesterday nor tomorrow. To enter deeply into this present moment is thus to plunge into eternity, to step through the looking glass and into the world of the Unborn and the Undying.

CW 1: *No Boundary*, 489

WHEN ALL things are nothing but God, there are then no things, and no God, but only *this*.

No objects, no subjects, only this. No entering this state, no leaving it; it is absolutely and eternally and always already the case: the simple feeling of being, the basic and simple immediacy of any and all states, prior to the four quadrants, prior to the split between inside and outside, prior to seer and seen, prior to the rise of worlds, ever-present as pure Presence, the simple feeling of being: empty awareness as the opening or clearing in which all worlds arise, ceaselessly: I-I is the box the universe comes in.

Abiding as I-I, the world arises as before,

but now there is no one to witness it. I-I is not "in here" looking "out there": there is no in here, no out there, only this. It is the radical end to all egocentrism, all geocentrism, all biocentrism, all sociocentrism, all theocentrism, because it is the radical end of all centrisms, period. It is the final *decentering* of all manifest realms, in all domains, at all times, in all places. As Dzogchen Buddhism would put it, because all phenomena are primordially empty, all phenomena, just as they are, are self-liberated as they arise.

In that pure empty awareness, I-I am the rise and fall of all worlds, ceaselessly, endlessly. I-I swallow the Kosmos and span the centuries, untouched by time or turmoil, embracing each with primordial purity, fierce compassion. It has never started, this nightmare of evolution, and therefore it will never end.

It is as it is, self-liberated at the moment of its very arising. And it is only *this*.

The All is I-I. I-I is Emptiness. Emptiness is freely manifesting. Freely manifesting is self-liberating.

Zen, of course, would put it all much more simply, and point directly to just *this*.

Still pond
A frog jumps in
Plop!

CW 6: *Sex, Ecology, Spirituality*, 318

ALWAYS ALREADY suffering death Now, we are always already living eternally. The search is always already over.

CW 1: *The Spectrum of Consciousness*, 373

NOT IN Emptiness, but as Emptiness, I am released from the fate of a never-ending addition of parts, and I stand free as the Source and Suchness of the glorious display.

I taste the sky and swallow whole the Kosmos, and nothing is added to me; I disappear in a million forms and nothing is subtracted; I rise as the sun to greet my own day, and nothing moves at all.

CW 6: *Sex, Ecology, Spirituality*, 532

WHAT CAUSES suffering is the grasping and desiring of the separate self, and what ends it is the meditative path that transcends self and desire. The point is that suffering is inherent in the knot or contraction known as self, and the only way to end suffering is to end the self. It's not that after enlightenment, or after spiritual practice in general, you no longer feel pain or anguish or fear or hurt. You do. It's simply that they no longer threaten your existence, and so they cease to be problematic. You are no longer identified with them, dramatizing them, energizing them, threatened by them. On the one hand, there is no longer any fragmented self to threaten, and on the other, the big Self can't be threatened since, being the All, there is nothing outside of it that could harm it. A profound relaxing and uncoiling occurs in the heart.

CW 5: *Grace and Grit*, 103–104

SUDDENLY, without any warning, at any time or place, with no apparent cause, it can happen.

CW 1: *No Boundary*, 433

WITH THE awakening of constant consciousness, you become something of a divine schizophrenic, in the popular sense of "split-minded," because you have access to *both* the Witness and the ego. You are actually "whole-minded," but it sounds like it's split, because you are aware of the constant

Witness or Spirit in you, and you are also perfectly aware of the movie of life, the ego and all its ups and downs. So you still feel pain and suffering and sorrow, but they can no longer convince you of their importance—you are no longer the victim of life, but its Witness.

In fact, because you are no longer afraid of your feelings, you can engage them with much greater intensity. The movie of life becomes more vivid and vibrant, precisely because you are no longer grasping or avoiding it, and thus no longer trying to dull or dilute it. You no longer turn the volume down. You might even cry harder, laugh louder, jump higher. Choiceless awareness doesn't mean you cease to feel; it means you feel fully, feel deeply, feel to infinity itself, and laugh and cry and love until it hurts. Life jumps right off the screen, and you are one with all of it, because you don't recoil.

CW 8: *One Taste*, 344–345

AND SO: given the measure of your own authentic realization, you were actually thinking about *gently whispering* into the ear of [the] near-deaf world? No, my friend, you must shout. Shout from the heart of what you have seen, shout however you can.

But not indiscriminately. Let us proceed carefully with this transformative shout. Let small pockets of radically transformative spirituality, authentic spirituality, focus their efforts, and transform their students. And let these pockets slowly, carefully, responsibly, humbly, begin to spread their influence, embracing an *absolute tolerance* for all views, but attempting nonetheless to advocate a true and authentic and integral spirituality—by example, by radiance, by obvious release, by unmistakable liberation. Let those pockets of transformation gently persuade the world and its reluctant selves, and challenge their legitimacy, and challenge their limiting translations, and offer an awakening in the face of the numbness that haunts the world at large.

Let it start right here, right now, with us—with you and with me—and with our commitment to breathe into infinity until infinity alone is the only statement that the world will recognize. Let a radical realization shine from our faces, and roar from our hearts, and thunder from our brains—this simple fact, this obvious fact: that you, in the very immediateness of your present awareness, are in fact the entire world, in all its frost and fever, in all its glories and its grace, in all its triumphs and its tears. You do not see the sun, you are the sun; you do not hear the rain, you are the rain; you do not feel the earth, you are the earth. And in that simple, clear, unmistakable regard, translation has ceased in all domains, and you have transformed into the very Heart of the Kosmos Itself—and there, right there, very simply, very quietly, it is all undone.

Wonder and remorse will then be alien to you, and self and others will be alien to you, and outside and inside will have no meaning at all. And in that obvious shock of recognition—where my Master is my Self, and that Self is the Kosmos at large, and the Kosmos is my Soul—you will walk very gently into the fog of this world, and transform it entirely by doing nothing at all.

And then, and then, and only then—you will finally, clearly, carefully and with compassion, write on the tombstone of a self that never even existed: There is only Spirit.

CW 8: *One Taste*, 312–313

EPILOGUE

LISTEN TO ME:

> *Everything is you.*
> *You are empty.*
> *Empty is freely manifesting.*
> *Freely manifesting is self liberating.*

Notice your present awareness. Notice the objects arising in your awareness—the images and thoughts arising in your mind, the feelings and sensations arising in your body, the myriad objects arising around you in the room or environment. All of these are objects arising in your awareness.

Now think about what was in your awareness 5 minutes ago. Most of the thoughts have changed, most of the bodily sensations have changed, and probably most of the environment has changed. But something has not changed. Something in you is the same now as it was 5 minutes ago. What is present now that was present 5 minutes ago?

I AMness. The feeling-awareness of I AMness is still present. I am that ever-present I AMness. That I AMness is present now, it was present a moment ago, it was present a minute ago, it was present 5 minutes ago.

What was present 5 hours ago?

I AMness. That sense of I AMness is an ongoing, self-knowing, self-recognizing, self-validating I AMness. It is present now, it was present 5 hours ago. All my thoughts have changed, all my bodily sensations have changed, my environment has changed, but I AM is ever-present, radiant, open, empty, clear, spacious, transparent, free. Objects have changed, but not this formless I AMness. This obvious and present I AMness is present now as it was present 5 hours ago.

What was present 5 years ago?

I AMness. So many objects have come and gone, so many feelings have come and gone, so many thoughts have come and gone, so many dramas and terrors and loves and hates have come, and stayed awhile, and gone. But one thing has not come, and one thing has not gone. What is that? What is the only thing present in your awareness right now that you can remember was present 5 years ago? This timeless, ever-present feeling of I AMness is present now as it was 5 years ago.

What was present 5 centuries ago?

All that is ever-present is I AMness. Every person feels this same I AMness— because it is not a body, it is not a thought, it is not an object, it is not the environment, it is not anything that can be seen, but rather is the ever-present Seer, the ongoing open and empty Witness of all that is arising, in any person, in any world, in any place, at any time, in all the worlds until the end of time, there is only and always this obvious and immediate I AMness. What else could you possibly know? What else does anybody ever know? There is only and always this radiant, self-knowing, self-feeling, self-transcending I AMness, whether present now, 5 minutes ago, 5 hours ago, 5 centuries ago.

5 millennia ago?

Before Abraham was, I AM. Before the universe was, I AM. This is my original Face, the face I had before my parents were born, the face I had before the universe was born, the Face I had for all eternity until I decided to play this round of hide and seek, and get lost in the objects of my own creation.

I will NEVER again pretend that I do not know or feel my own I AMness.

And with that, the game is undone. A

million thoughts have come and gone, a million feelings have come and gone, a million objects have come and gone. But one thing has not come, and one thing has not gone: the great Unborn and the great Undying, which never enters or leaves the stream of time, a pure Presence above time, floating in eternity. I am this great, obvious, self-knowing, self-validating, self-liberating I AMness.

Before Abraham was, I AM.

I AM is none other than Spirit in 1st-person, the ultimate, the sublime, the radiant all-creating Self of the entire Kosmos, present in me and you and him and her and them—as the I AMness that each and every one of us feels.

Because in all the known universes, the overall number of I AMs is but one.

Rest as I AMness always, the exact I AMness you feel right now, which is Unborn Spirit itself shining in and as you. Assume your personal identity as well—as this or that object, or this or that self, or this and that thing—resting always in the Ground of it All, as this great and completely obvious I AMness, and get up and go on about your day, in the universe I AM created.

It's a new day, it's a new dawn, it's a new man, it's a new woman. The new human is integral, and so is the new world.

The Integral Vision, 221–225

SOURCES

All material from books previously published by Shambhala Publications has been reprinted by arrangement with Shambhala Publications, Inc., Boston, www.shambhala.com.

BOOKS

The Atman Project: A Transpersonal View of Human Development. 2nd ed. Wheaton, IL: Quest Books / Theosophical Publishing House, 1996. © 1996 by Ken Wilber. Selections reprinted from *The Collected Works of Ken Wilber*, vol. 2. Boston: Shambhala Publications, 1999. © 1999 by Ken Wilber.

Boomeritis: A Novel That Will Set You Free. Boston: Shambhala Publications, 2002. © 2002 by Ken Wilber.

A Brief History of Everything. Boston: Shambhala Publications, 1996. © 1996 by Ken Wilber. Selections reprinted from *The Collected Works of Ken Wilber*, vol. 7. Boston: Shambhala Publications, 2000. © 1999 by Ken Wilber.

The Eye of Spirit: An Integral Vision for a World Gone Slightly Mad. Boston: Shambhala Publications, 1997. © 1997 by Ken Wilber. Selections reprinted from *The Collected Works of Ken Wilber*, vol. 7. Boston: Shambhala Publications, 2000. © 1999 by Ken Wilber.

Eye to Eye: The Quest for the New Paradigm. Boston: Shambhala Publications, 1996. © 1983, 1990, 1996 by Ken Wilber. Selections reprinted from *The Collected Works of Ken Wilber*, vol. 3. Boston: Shambhala Publications, 1999. © 1999 by Ken Wilber.

Grace and Grit: Spirituality and Healing in the Life and Death of Treya Killam Wilber. Boston: Shambhala Publications, 1991. © Selections reprinted from *The Collected Works of Ken Wilber*, vol. 5. Boston: Shambhala Publications, 2000. © 2000 by Ken Wilber.

Integral Psychology: Consciousness, Spirit, Psychology, Therapy. Boston: Shambhala Publications, 2000. © 2000 by Ken Wilber. Selections reprinted from *The Collected Works of Ken Wilber*, vol. 4. Boston: Shambhala Publications, 1999. © 1999 by Ken Wilber.

Integral Spirituality: A Startling New Role for Religion in the Modern and Postmodern World. Boston: Integral Books, 2006. © 2006 by Ken Wilber.

The Integral Vision: A Very Short Introduction to the Revolutionary Integral Approach to Life, God, the Universe, and Everything. Boston: Shambhala Publications, 2007. © 2007 by Ken Wilber.

The Marriage of Sense and Soul: Integrating Science and Religion. New York: Random House, 1998. © 1998 by Ken Wilber.

Works of Ken Wilber, vol. 4. Boston: Shambhala Publications, 1999. © 1999 by Ken Wilber.

Sex, Ecology, Spirituality: The Spirit of Evolution. 2nd ed. Boston: Shambhala Publications, 2000. © 1995, 2000 by Ken Wilber. Selections reprinted from *The Collected Works of Ken Wilber*, vol. 6. Boston: Shambhala Publications, 2000. © 2000 by Ken Wilber.

A Sociable God: Toward a New Understanding of Religion. Boston: Shambhala Publications, 1984. © 1983, 1984 by Ken Wilber. Selections reprinted from *The Collected Works of Ken Wilber*, vol. 3. Boston: Shambhala Publications, 1999. © 1999 by Ken Wilber.

The Spectrum of Consciousness. 2nd ed. Wheaton, IL: Quest Books / Theosophical Publishing House, 1993. © 1993 by Ken Wilber. Selections reprinted from *The Collected Works of Ken Wilber*, vol. 1. Boston:

Shambhala Publications, 1999. © 1999 by Ken Wilber.

A Theory of Everything: An Integral Vision for Business, Politics, Science and Spirituality. Boston: Shambhala Publications, 2000. © 2000 by Ken Wilber.

Up from Eden: A Transpersonal View of Human Evolution. Wheaton, IL: Quest Books / Theosophical Publishing House 1996. © 1981, 1996 by Ken Wilber. Selections reprinted from *The Collected Works of Ken Wilber*, vol. 2. Boston: Shambhala Publications, 1999. © 1999 by Ken Wilber.

OTHER SOURCES

"Death, Rebirth, and Meditation." Selections reprinted from *The Collected Works of Ken Wilber*, vol. 4. Boston: Shambhala Publications, 1999. © 1999 by Ken Wilber. Originally published in Gary Doore (ed.), *What Survives?: Contemporary Explorations of*

Life after Death. Los Angeles: Jeremy P. Tarcher, 1990. © 1990 by Ken Wilber.

Foreword to Andrew Cohen, *Living Enlightenment: A Call for Evolution Beyond Ego*. Lenox, MA: Moksha Press, 2002.

Foreword to David Deida, *Finding God through Sex: A Spiritual Guide to Ecstatic Loving and Deep Passion for Men and Women*. London: Plexus Publishing, 2002.

Foreword to Frank Visser, *Ken Wilber: Thought as Passion*. Albany: SUNY Press, 2003.

"The Guru and the Pandit: The Evolution of Enlightenment, Andrew Cohen and Ken Wilber in Dialogue," *What Is Enlightenment?* no. 21 (Spring/Summer 2002), 38–49, 136–143.

"In the Eye of the Artist: Art and the Perennial Philosophy." Foreword to Alex Grey, Ken Wilber, and Carlo McCormick, *Sacred*

RESOURCES

www.kenwilber.com: Ken's newest writings, blogs, photos, videos, and more.

www.integrallife.com: The definitive portal to an Integral life.

www.integralinstitute.org: The "Multiplex" of all Integral activities.

www.integralnaked.org: Exclusive Integral audio and video content.

www.integralspiritualcenter.org: The finest spiritual teachers in the world.

www.myilp.com: Learn about Integral Life Practice.

Library of Congress
Cataloging-in-Publication Data

The pocket Ken Wilber /
compiled and edited by Colin Bigelow.
— 1st ed.
   p.   cm.
Includes bibliographical references.
ISBN 978-1-59030-637-6 (pbk.: alk. paper)
1. Wilber, Ken. I. Bigelow, Colin.
   BF109.W54P63 2008
      191—dc22
      2008015064

SHAMBHALA POCKET CLASSICS

THE ART OF PEACE:
Teachings of the Founder of Aikido
by Morihei Ueshiba
Compiled and translated by John Stevens

THE ART OF WAR by Sun Tzu
Translated by Thomas Cleary

THE ART OF WORLDLY WISDOM
by Baltasar Gracián

AWAKENING LOVING-KINDNESS
by Pema Chödrön

THE BOOK OF FIVE RINGS
by Miyamoto Musashi
Translated by Thomas Cleary

TEACHINGS OF THE BUDDHA
Edited by Jack Kornfield

THOUGHTS IN SOLITUDE
by Thomas Merton

THE TIBETAN BOOK OF THE DEAD
Translated by Francesca Fremantle
and Chögyam Trungpa

WRITING DOWN THE BONES
by Natalie Goldberg

ZEN LESSONS:
The Art of Leadership
Translated by Thomas Cleary